Always Remember:

IF IT AIN'T FUN, IT AIN'T WORTH DOING!

By
Wayne Kehl

PublishAmerica
Baltimore

© 2006 by Wayne Kehl.
All rights reserved. No part of this book may be reproduced, stored in a retrieval system or transmitted in any form or by any means without the prior written permission of the publishers, except by a reviewer who may quote brief passages in a review to be printed in a newspaper, magazine or journal.

First printing

All characters appearing in this work are fictitious. Any resemblance to real persons, living or dead, is purely coincidental.

At the specific preference of the author, PublishAmerica allowed this work to remain exactly as the author intended, verbatim, without editorial input.

ISBN: 1-59286-115-6
PUBLISHED BY PUBLISHAMERICA, LLLP
www.publishamerica.com
Baltimore

Printed in the United States of America

Dedication

I dedicate this book to Kevin Wolfe of Leadersway Inc. (www.Leadersway.com).

Kevin is my coach, mentor, friend and inspiration. He is at the top of his game in the leadership and management consulting field and is perhaps, one of the most inspirational motivational speakers working in North America today.

Kevin changed my life. It is because of his recognition of my skill and desire to be a writer that I finished this book. Without his encouragement and cajoling, my manuscript might never have made it to print. Without his coaching and friendship, I might never have had the words to fill the pages.

Kevin, this book is for you...The rest are for me, my friend.

Cheers!
Wayne Kehl

Introduction

It is with humility and deep respect for a dear friend and talented writer that I am introducing a book that every business owner, leader and manager must read. Throughout the years as a Business Coach and Professional Speaker, I have had the privilege of reading the absolute best in leadership and management books. For me there are two qualities that determine value. *First,* the book has to connect with what is happening NOW! Too many of the "best sellers" miss the mark when it comes to addressing the most pressing issues facing today's leaders and managers. Face it; many authors are disconnected from the real world of business and care more about selling books then making a difference. *Second,* the book has to clearly identify and set in play tangible action steps that can be applied right away. Here's a question for you; "how many highly recommended leadership/management books have you read that didn't result in you taking action?" And by the way, if what you read doesn't result in action, where is the value? I don't know about you but there are plenty of ways I can spend my time that make a lot more sense than reading a book that I don't get!

"Always Remember: If It Ain't Fun, It Ain't Worth Doing!" is a book that I am thrilled to report is not only packed full of value, it exceeded my two defining qualities by a long shot! In the book, Wayne does a masterful job of identifying the most significant challenge facing business owners today; engaging disengaged employees. We have been working for years to learn what it will take to bring out the best in people. We have been working for years to learn what leaders and managers must do to realize the largely untapped talent of the workforce. Wayne, and his life like characters not only identify the most significant challenges in business today, they go one step further; they give you everything you need to take action. Read the book, lay out your action plan and make sure everyone in your organization that will benefit gets their chance as well. Take it from someone who is in the current of the business world everyday. This stuff works, it applies and will make you a better leader or manager for your people!

I'll leave the rest of the lessons to you and your journey through *"Always Remember: If It Ain't Fun, It Ain't Worth Doing!"* but I do want to leave you with what made the book special for me. As a Business/ Executive coach, I have had the most amazing gift of meeting and working with some incredibly successful people. Wayne is no exception. Above all, I have learned that each one of these people share two qualities that I have found consistent in all successful people:

Energy and Passion!

Guess what? Energy and passion are no accident and are the qualities that absolutely bring out the best in people. You've seen people who have it, you've worked with people who have it and if you are one of the fortunate ones you've followed someone who has it! The secret is in the title; *"If it ain't fun, it ain't worth doing!"* People who are full of energy and passion are people who get up every day doing what they love to do and do well. So there you go! The end goal is in sight. Now read the book to learn what it will take to get you there!

With that said, I want to extend my heartfelt congratulations to my friend for life, Wayne Kehl. For those of us who have had the privilege of working, playing and spending time with Wayne, it is clear to all of us that he has found his Energy and Passion! Now that he has found his…go and find yours!

Life is good…

Kevin Wolfe
LeadersWay Inc.
Business/Executive Coaching
Talent Management

Table of Contents

Foreword 11

Chapter 1
The Formative Years 13

Chapter 2
The Young Insurance Man 21

Chapter 3
Shelton Saunderson 40

Chapter 4
Management Chaos 45

Chapter 5
Joshua's Tire Center 57

Chapter 6
Start at the Beginning 65

Chapter 7
Earn Your Stripes 76

Chapter 8
You Are My Manager...Not My Friend 84

Chapter 9
If I Can't Be Happy, Neither Can You 94

Chapter 10
We Need to Talk 104

Chapter 11
The Essential Trait of Successful Managers 112

Chapter 12
Minders and Finders 121

Chapter 13
Clear Expectations 132

Chapter 14
If It Ain't Fun, It Ain't Worth Doing 148

Chapter 15
The End 153

Chapter 16
A New Beginning 160

Foreword

This is a story about a young manager trying desperately to make a difference in his workplace. Like many new managers, he cannot understand why so many of the people that work for him are unhappy.

This scenario plays itself out in offices and other workplaces all over North America everyday. Individuals are often promoted to management for the wrong reasons. Some are promoted due to their success in sales or their tenure with their firms. Others are brought in from the outside when a company has run out of potential managers to promote from within. In these situations, real skills are often overlooked in favor of education or job history. Many managers fail to understand the impact of their personal management style on the long-term success of their business. All but the best-run offices have some or all of the problems discussed in this book.

I have been in business for 35 years and in management for 25 of those. I have never been formally trained but I have read dozens of books and been to hundreds of seminars and training sessions in my effort to become a better manager. I have read books about *fish, cheese, frogs and monkeys*. I have learned about *presents, illusions and fans who rave*. I have been to seminars on selling, coaching, and behavioral styles. As great as all of that information was, I found that the best training came from my own personal observations and experiences at the office.

I wanted to write a readable and interesting book about management while telling a story that anyone in any walk of life could identify with. This book is a distillation of experiences and lessons from my own life. It chronicles the trials and tribulations of Walter Kennedy as he battles the challenges of management in a large office. Like me, he has had no formal training but he has a desire to learn. He is fortunate to find a mentor in Joshua O'Hare, a successful tire dealer who sees a little of himself in Walter and wants to help.

As the story unfolds, Walter will learn that **FUN** is the essential element of a successful business. Through the course of his travails he learns what *"If it ain't fun, it ain't worth doing"* really means.

This book is for anyone who wants to learn more about the differences between great and mediocre managers. Every person at any level who works in an office or any typical hierarchical management system will be able to identify with the characters and situations discussed on these pages.

I hope you enjoy the reading as much as I enjoyed the writing.

Wayne Kehl

www.waynekehl.com

Chapter 1

The Formative Years

Walter Kennedy was borne the youngest son of Dale and Martha Kennedy, a typical middle class couple who lived in a normal middle class neighborhood in Spruce River, Ontario. He had one brother Bill, who had been borne four years before him.

As Walter grew it was clear to everyone that he was a happy child with a twinkle in his eye and bit of mischief in his heart. Even as an adolescent, it was overwhelmingly clear that Walter was someone that people would always want to be around. He was a handsome lad with a winning smile and healthy mop of wavy hair. Everyone loved his active sense of humor and Walter had a lot of friends because of it. His desire to be the center of attention detracted from his studies however, and throughout his schooling he was a mediocre student. He got into trouble with his teachers from time to time and they often told his parents that Walter wasn't living up to his full potential. Brother Bill on the other hand, was more serious and although he had few friends, he garnered a lot of attention from his parents by bringing home excellent grades and accolades from his teachers.

Walter and Bill had little in common, and tended to avoid each other. Bill studied while Walter played. Walter visited with his friends while Bill read. When the two brothers did have time together, it usually didn't go well. Walter harbored a secret resentment for Bill's scholastic ability and did everything he could to overwhelm his parents with his humor and mischief in order to avoid being compared to him. Brother Bill on the other hand, took great joy in bragging about his latest scholastic award or good report card. That appeared to Walter to be an effort to belittle him in the eyes of Dale and Martha. In later years Walter would realize that Bill was merely seeking some of the attention that was so lavishly heaped upon his younger brother.

Unbeknownst to Bill, he was inadvertently assisting in building the foundation of a successful future career for Walter with his excellent performance and superior attitude. As a teenager, Walter knew that he could get attention by being funny but he was also smart enough to know that he couldn't survive as an adult unless he had skills like Bill. While Bill was leafing through University brochures, Walter was pondering his future. Should he be a mechanic? He always liked tinkering with cars. Should he work as a logger as so many of his friends were planning to do? Or, should he put his head before his heart and go to University as Bill had done before him.

High school graduation day for Bill began his arduous journey through a web of never ending scholastic trials. Although he arrived at University with great grades, he had absolutely no idea what he wanted to do with his life. He went from one major to the next and ended up with a Bachelor's degree that turned out to be of almost no more value than his high school diploma. Walter was determined not to be like Bill. He rejected the idea of attending a University. He was going to be a logger when he finished high school. Jobs were plentiful and no experience or training was required. He found a job almost immediately after graduation.

Spruce River was a town of sixty thousand people approximately 300 miles North of Toronto. The main source of revenue for the community was the forest industry. Those who weren't directly involved in harvesting or milling of trees provided services to the forest industry. It was a natural evolution for the young men of the community to gravitate toward the relatively high paying logging sector immediately after high school.

Logging got Walter out into the woods where he loved to be. He had grown up fishing and hunting with his Dad and always loved the peaceful environment of the forest. It also brought him near many of his high school friends who were there before him. This was good honest work, he thought. He often said, "Real men work in the woods; only sissies go to University." He didn't really believe that, but it gave him an opportunity to reinforce his decision to go in the opposite direction of Bill.

Walter found the thing he liked best about logging was the interaction with the other men. There was always a joke amongst friends and a pat on the back from the older guys. It had the same atmosphere as high school except that pens and books were replaced by chain saws and logging trucks. If he did something wrong, the other loggers had no qualms about telling Walter in no uncertain terms that he had screwed up and had better not do it again. He was never offended by these admonishments as he knew the work was dangerous and the other guys were only looking out for his safety and that of his co-workers. In the logging industry, one mistake could mean death.

Walter's favorite co-worker was an elderly Native fellow named Buffalo Johnson. Buffalo liked Walter's sense of humor, his work ethic, and his desire to learn. He took Walter under his wing and taught him the wisdom and decorum of the logging camp. He taught him how to tell the difference between "white rot," "red rot," "dry rot," and "wet rot." One must always know what kind of rot is present at the base of a tree in order to know how much of it to cut off without wasting any of the good wood further up the trunk. He taught Walter never to undercut a line of trees in a row and then knock them down all at once in a "domino effect." That tactic had gained popularity in the woods as it saved a lot of time. Unfortunately, it had also caused the death of many a good man when one of the trees hung up on another and had to be taken down very precariously or had simply fallen in the wrong spot. Trees deserved respect and had to be cut down one at a time.

Trees with a pronounced curve in the trunk caused by damage during the seedling stage were called *"barber's Chairs."* These had to be handled carefully. Trees that

ALWAYS REMEMBER: IF IT AIN'T FUN, IT AIN'T WORTH DOING

forked out into two trunks at the base were called *"schoolmarms."* These had to be approached with equal caution. Walter listened intently to Buffalo's teachings. He sensed that these lessons were more than mere logging techniques, but something deeper that might serve him well later in life.

Buffalo's most critical advice had to do with people. He taught Walter the *pecking order* of the crew. The older guys commanded the greatest degree of respect. At dinner time in the cookhouse, they were first in line. This wasn't written down anywhere, it was just assumed. When you passed one of them in an active logging area or on a trail, you greeted them with a smile and a cheerful, *"howdy"* no matter what your mood was. When they told you to move, you moved. These fellows knew the woods and they knew what they were doing better than anyone else. They also had respect for the young guys coming up and they were willing to assist them so that they could live long fruitful lives and become *old loggers* too. Buffalo convinced Walter that as he grew in experience, he must pass along his respect and wisdom to those that followed him into the industry. This wasn't just courtesy on Buffalo's part...it was life and death. In the forest industry hazards are everywhere and everyone must look out for everyone else. Most importantly, Buffalo taught Walter that being nice was a lot easier than not and a smile would get him a lot further with the crew than a frown, any day of the week.

Walter certainly learned how to log but what he really learned was how to follow the rules and how to get along with the other members of the crew. He realized that he enjoyed being part of a team and had quickly learned the skills to work in that environment. Those early lessons would stay with him forever.

As time passed, Walter grew tired of logging. It was brutally cold in the woods in the wintertime and excruciatingly hot in the summer. The hours were long and the work was backbreaking. The pay was good, but the time spent in the camp, far away from family and friends negated any joy that his income would bring. Walter had met a very special girl his last year in high school and he longed for an opportunity to get to know her better. He also felt that he could do more with his life. As much as he admired and respected his fellow loggers, he saw himself as a captain of industry rather than a crewman. With no job to go to, nor a University degree to fall back on, Walter picked up his final paycheck, said good bye to Buffalo and moved back to his hometown. Buffalo's parting comment was, "Good for you boy, get out of this place and do something with your life. You're gonna be somebody some day." As much as Walter knew that Buffalo was only trying to give him an encouraging send off, he never forgot those words.

When he arrived back at his parent's home, Walter had not had a haircut in months and had not shaved for almost as long. When he walked through the door his Dad, Dale said, "You look like Heck son. What have they been doing to you out there?"

"You know Dad. You used to work in the bush when you were a kid," Walter retorted.

"Yah, and I never liked it much either. Remember what I always say, *"If it ain't fun, it ain't worth doing,"* Dale stated with a smile. "Why don't you clean yourself up and come to work for me in my office?"

ALWAYS REMEMBER: IF IT AIN'T FUN, IT AIN'T WORTH DOING

Dale was a strong and determined individual. He was the epitome of a self-made man. He had less than a high school education when he left his family farm at only 16 years of age. He had served time in the Second World War as an infantryman and was wounded by a German hand grenade. Although he was an exceptional soldier, he took little pleasure in warfare, and was pleased to accept an honorable discharge at the end of it all. With very little education and no formal training, his career opportunities were limited. Fortunately, after the war there was a lot of work for laborers as the economy began ramping back up into full production. After working at various labor jobs, Dale found himself selling books for a living. Books were tough to sell door to door so he tried vacuum cleaners. After many door-slamming episodes, Dale studied for his real estate license and began selling houses. That job lead him to insurance sales, as the firm he worked for sold both real estate and insurance.

Dale found that he had a knack for insurance and quite liked the technical side of it. It was much easier to sell than real estate since very few people needed a new house, but almost everyone needed insurance every year. He worked hard and enjoyed a great deal of success until one day his boss came to him and asked him to take on the management of a small office in the North. Always up for a challenge, with hardly a second thought he packed up his young family and moved to Spruce River. After 5 years as a very successful manager with that firm Dale decided to go it alone and opened his own insurance agency. The business had flourished and now he needed a full time partner. He had tried partnerships in the past without success. Previous partners were never compatible for one reason or another. Dale hoped that his son Walter would be the one who would take on a big piece of his workload on a long-term basis. His wish was about to be granted.

Walter went to bed that night pondering his future again. He still wanted more than a simple logger's life. "Should I go back to the woods and move up the ladder with the logging company?" he asked himself. "Maybe I could become a forestry superintendent. Or should I go to work for Dad?" Working in an insurance office had never been his dream but it might afford him the opportunity to move on to greater things.

After a long and sleepless night Walter awoke with a new direction in life. He had decided to get a shave and a haircut, buy a suit and report for work at "Kennedy Insurance Services." This was the start of an odyssey that would change his life.

Chapter 2

The Young Insurance Man

Kennedy Insurance Services was a small office with a staff of four, including Dale. Walter's presence increased the count to five. That change was greeted with mixed reviews by the existing staff. Two of the younger ladies took to Walter right away. With his quick wit and affable charm, he stole their hearts and had them eating out of his hand in no time. Another staff member would not be so easy.

An older lady, Nora Johnston grumbled to the other staff that Walter was excess baggage and would only cut into the profit. She voiced this opinion to Dale but was soundly rebuked. Dale explained that he wanted to retire soon and needed to have his son there to learn the ropes and take over one day. He also told her that he expected her to train Walter and to get along with him. Nora wasn't really concerned about the office profit. Nor did she have any ambition to take over the office. She secretly felt that young Walter was a threat to her position and might want to force her out. She had worked hard over a ten-year period to become Dale's *right arm* and feared that she might lose her position of strength with him. Dale's motives were much more pure than she knew. He loved his son and truly wanted him to take over his business. He was an old-fashioned guy and in his heart, family succession was the natural course of things. Despite his respect for her, Nora had not even entered his mind when he made the decision to bring Walter on Board.

Walter sensed that he needed to get into Nora's good graces. Despite the fact that she was cold and aloof toward him, he knew that she was the undisputed office leader. She knew the business and she knew how everything worked. Most importantly she knew the clients and they all seemed to love her. Walter decided that she would be his mentor. She was to be his new "Buffalo" and he must find a way to be accepted by her.

One morning, after several weeks of cool treatment, Walter steeled himself, walked up to Nora's desk and asked her to have a closed-door discussion with him.

Nora, barely glancing up from her desk responded, "I'm too busy right now…maybe later." Unflinchingly, Walter pressed her for a specific time.

When the agreed upon time arrived, Nora walked stiffly and silently into Walter's office staring directly into his eyes in an obvious attempt to intimidate him. Walter smiled and calmly and quietly asked her to sit down. His voice cracked and wavered as he began to speak.

"Nora, I sense that you don't like me much," he said. Nora remained silent.

Frustrated by her lack of response, Walter began again, "Okay then, Nora let's assume that perhaps you might not like me. The problem I have is that I like you. And more importantly, I respect you. You have all of the skills and talents that I don't have. You are what makes this office run and without your help, I will never amount to anything."

Nora was taken aback by his candor. She was still suspicious of his motives, but her ego was bursting as she felt a swell of pride and self respect from Walter's comments. His obvious need for acceptance had broken down her defenses and she felt the need to open up to him.

"Look here, Walter," Nora began, "It's not that I don't like you. Frankly I think you are too young for this business and I have neither the time nor the desire to try to train you. I know that your Dad wants you here, but he always expects me to train the new people and he forgets that I already have a huge workload. It's just not fair!"

Walter could feel the raw emotion in Nora's words and sensed that she might begin weeping. He was never very good at dealing with people in tears so he picked up on her thought by saying, "I know it's not fair Nora. I agree with you. Dad should have thought more about this before he brought me on staff, but now it's too late. We can't turn back the clock so the only thing we can do now is work together. Can we do that please?" He followed his question with a kind, slow smile that gradually grew into a toothy grin.

Nora wasn't sure if it was Walter's audacity or his

infectious smile that got her started, but she began to laugh. That started Walter laughing and the two of them giggled and laughed together for several seconds.

As suddenly as Nora had begun to laugh, she stopped. She leaned across the desk, looked Walter square in the eyes and said, "You are a charmer aren't you. You sure take after your Dad on that account." Walter blushed at her directness. Sensing his vulnerability she said, "Okay then, Walter…let's do it. If you do as I tell you, and if you work your little tail off, we will become the best of friends."

"Thank you, thank you, and thank you! I knew you would be my Buffalo!" Walter exclaimed. As soon as he said it, he wished he could take it back.

"What the Heck is that supposed to mean?" Nora shouted.

"Sorry Nora, it's just that I had a good friend named Buffalo out in the logging camp who helped me and taught me everything I needed to know about logging. He was smart like you and I don't think I would have survived without him," Walter sputtered.

Nora relaxed and settled back into her chair. "That's high praise indeed Walter. I assume you are talking about Buffalo Johnson. That man is one of the smartest loggers around," she purred. "Let's see if I can teach you to be as good an insurance man as you were a logger. But don't *ever* call me Buffalo again!"

"Not a problem ma'am," Walter stated respectfully. "Can I call you Nora?" he asked.

"Naturally," she replied. With that, Nora got up from her chair, spun around and strutted toward the door. As she reached the door she turned around, gave Walter a wink and said again, "You *are* a charmer." Nora was happy now. She was confident that her position was safe and besides, "It might be kind of fun to train this young pup," she thought.

As soon as Nora was gone Walter knew that his early training with his old friend Buffalo had already had a positive effect on his new career. Had he not learned the need for respect for his elders and how to use his smile to his advantage, he might not have had this breakthrough. He knew too that what he was learning on the job could not be taught in schools. He needed experience and he needed to learn how to use all of his natural skills and intelligence to survive in the business world. Nora was his first success.

With Nora's help Walter was learning the ropes of the insurance business. She started him at the bottom doing filing and emptying waste paper baskets. Walter did this work without complaint even though he longed to get into the meat of the business and start dealing with clients. The time that Nora spent with Walter was not only valuable but it was a great lesson for the future. He learned the value of mentoring and it became clear to him that new employees need time and training with a seasoned hand in order to become comfortable in the workplace. Ultimately, this early training allows them to master their craft. It also gave Nora the opportunity to observe problems as they occurred and point her young charge in the right direction.

Walter had been furiously studying his insurance examination manual every night. He knew that he could not begin acting as an agent until he had his insurance license. In the mean time he watched and listened to Nora and his Dad while trying to remember everything they did. As he watched them work he admired many of their methods but imagined ways to improve upon some of them He was building himself up to be the best insurance broker the world had ever seen. He had accepted this as his new career and he was determined to be successful.

Exam day arrived at last. Walter strolled into the exam room with the conviction of a samurai. He opened the envelope that contained the exam booklet and scanned the questions. "Cool!" he thought, "I know the answers to every single one of these questions."

Walter quickly and confidently answered all of the questions, comfortable in the knowledge that he had aced the exam. He waited with anticipation for three weeks until the envelope with his results arrived. "Yes!" he yelled as he read the form. He had scored ninety eight percent. He ran into his Dad's office waiving the paper furiously. "I passed, I passed, and I got a ninety eight, Dad!" he exclaimed.

His dad looked up from the file he was working on and with a big smile on his face said, "I knew you weren't as dumb as those teachers in school said you were." With that, Dale came around from behind his desk, embraced Walter, and said, "This is just the beginning son. I am very proud of you today and I know that we will see even greater things from you in the future." Dale then broke out of the embrace so that his son wouldn't see the tears beginning to well up in his eyes. He walked over to his door and yelled, "Hey Nora, did you hear about Walter's exam marks?"

Nora, having heard the commotion was already on her way over to Dale's office. She hugged Walter and whispered, "Charming, and a brain too. You have made us all very proud today, young man."

After closing up that night, the entire staff along with Dale and Martha took Walter out for a celebratory dinner in Spruce River's finest restaurant. Dale gave a speech congratulating Walter and thanking the staff for helping his son with his studies. His manner was unusually subdued that night. It was almost like a passing of the torch for Dale. He realized that his boy had become a man and that soon he would be able to take over the business. It was a bittersweet joy for him as he was just now coming to grips with the fact that he was almost sixty years old and had to start thinking about retirement.

Walter wasted no time progressing through his apprenticeship. The next five years would be spent learning the technical side of the business. He immediately began his studies with the Insurance Institute so that he could learn everything there was to know about the technicalities of commercial and personal insurance. That program required that he pass twelve courses of study in separate disciplines. He achieved high marks on all of the exams and passed with honors. He acquired the gold medal for top graduating marks in Canada that year and was thrilled to be recognized as one of the top students in the history of the program. He then studied for his life insurance license and passed that one in record time. Walter had become a true professional insurance person and he had the credentials to prove it.

When he wasn't studying, Walter was selling. He became an expert general insurance and bonding agent. He focussed a lot of his energy on insuring his first love, the logging industry. On one of his trips into the woods to visit one of his logging clients, he was surprised and thrilled to see his old friend Buffalo marching into camp carrying his chain saw over his shoulder. It had been over five years since he laid eyes on his mentor. He ran out of his client's office and raced across the yard to greet him. Buffalo looked up when he saw Walter coming toward him and raised his massive hand in a gesture intended to slow him down. It didn't work. Walter threw himself at Buffalo and wrapped his arms around his body, giving him a massive bear hug. That was quite a shock to the old logger. "Whoa there, young fella and let me get my breath," Buffalo groaned. He stepped back from Walter and surveyed the well-dressed man before him. "By God, you do look like something, don't you?" he exclaimed with a smile. "I knew you would make it some day."

Walter grabbed Buffalo by the arm saying, "I'm so glad to see you old pal and I have so much to tell you." The two of them spent the next 3 hours reminiscing about their days together and swapping stories about their current situations.

Finally Walter had to return to the city and he gave his friend another big hug before he turned toward his car. Buffalo said, "Thanks for remembering me, Walter. I would have thought that you would have forgotten about a sorry old logger after this length of time."

Walter was quick to respond, "No way my friend. You have been more of an influence on me than you will ever know. I don't think I will ever forget you."

"That's nice," Buffalo said with a sigh. The two of them shook hands and Walter climbed into his car, knowing that it was time to head back home to be with his new

wife. As Walter's car motored out of the yard, Buffalo yelled after him, "Watch out for barber's chairs and schoolmarms, my friend!"
"I always do!" Walter yelled back.

* * *

Walter and his wife Lydia had 2 children; a boy named Jeremy and his younger sister Joanie. The kids were borne four years apart, just like Walter and his brother Bill. Walter always wondered if the kids would turn out like his brother and him. Would they have such diverse personalities? Later in life Walter would learn that they were quite different, but in the case of Jeremy and Joanie, the younger sibling would be the quiet, studious one and his son Jeremy would be just like him. The kids were his life. Although he always loved his work, it became a means to and end that allowed him to give the kids the things they needed and wanted. He would never lose sight of his responsibilities toward his children no matter how successful he became.

Walter's career continued to progress and improve as his reputation in the industry soared. He received a lot of job offers but turned them all down in favor of working for Dale. He owed his Dad everything and his strong sense of loyalty would not allow him to let the old man down. He had no idea that as Dale neared his sixty-fifth birthday he was going to ask Walter to make the biggest decision of his life.

One morning, Dale surprised Walter by coming into his office, closing the door and sitting down in one of Walter's client chairs. That had never happened before.

In the past when Dale came into to Walter's office, he never closed the door and he was never there long enough to sit down. Walter knew something was up and he wondered what might be wrong. Dale had a serious, yet calm look on his face and was not speaking. Walter needed to break the silence and said quietly, "What's up Dad?"

Dale looked at Walter for a second without speaking, and then said, "I want to retire, son." Walter's mind began to race. If his Dad was going to retire, what was he going to do? What was he supposed to say now? Should he simply acknowledge the statement or should he protest it. He always knew that it was his Dad's intention to have him take over the business but he had never prepared himself for the day that it would actually happen. The two men observed each other silently for what seemed an eternity. Finally, Walter spoke.

"Okay Dad, I guess we both knew this day was coming. What do we do now?" He asked.

Dale smiled and said, "Don't look so serious, son. This is a good thing. I know that you are ready for this, and I am certainly ready for retirement. I want you to buy me out and take over the business."

Walter was stunned. "Buy him out?" he thought. Walter was mentally reviewing his bank balances and outstanding debts. He knew that it was his turn to speak, but he couldn't think of anything to say at that moment.

Dale could see that his announcement was not going over as well as he had hoped. Fortunately, he was a wily old bird and he had already thought of all of the options. Walter could acquire a loan to purchase Dale's shares in the firm. Dale had given Walter a large number of shares a couple of years ago in order to justify his partnership. He could use those shares as collateral for a loan and take a second mortgage on his house. That would be enough to give Dale an immediate pay out. It would also leave Walter with a huge debt that would take many years to pay off. The second option would be that Walter could pay Dale off over time. That would mean that Dale would have to wait several years to recover all of his money, but it would allow Walter the ability to carry on running the business without damaging his credit rating. It would still however, mean a long-term debt. The final option was that they could sell the business to someone else and Walter could go to work for them. This last option was the least attractive to Dale as it would mean the end of Kennedy Insurance Services. However, it would allow him to retire in comfort and allow Walter to continue to progress in his career, free of any financial encumbrance. Dale described the options to Walter and then sat back in his chair saying, "Okay son, it's up to you now. What do you want to do?"

Walter was now even more dumfounded than he had been immediately after Dale's announcement. What to do? What to do? Finally he spoke, "Let me think about it would you Dad? This is a really big decision and for the life of me, I have no idea what I should do." Dale nodded and told Walter that he would like to be finished and on his way within 6 months, so there was lots of time. "Lots of time indeed," thought Walter.

Walter had a pensive drive home that night. He was oblivious to the other cars on the road and paid little attention to the speed limit signs. Immediately after walking through the door of his house he went to the fridge, pulled out a cold beer and listened to the pop and hiss as he pulled the tab on the can. He always kept beer glasses in the freezer, so he took one out and listened to the hollow ringing sound as he set it on the granite counter. As he poured the bubbling, golden liquid into the glass, he listened intently to the glop, glop sound as the glass filled up. With his frosty glass firmly in his hand, he sat on the couch and stared at the ceiling, saying nothing. When his wife Lydia came up from the basement where she was working on a new craft project, she asked him what was wrong. She could see the distress on his face.

Walter just grunted and said, "I don't know." He couldn't bring himself to discuss this life-changing event even with Lydia at this time. As always, he relied on his imagination and his past experience to walk him through all of the repercussions of all of the options. "Buy it and pay the bank, buy it and pay Dad, or sell it to someone else. What to do?" he thought to himself.

His mind wandered back to his time in the logging camp. What would Buffalo tell him to do? He recalled those days with a sense of serenity and joy. Those were simpler days when money wasn't an issue and every day was an adventure. Dry rot, wet rot, white rot, red rot, barber's chairs, schoolmarms! How could he use Buffalo's teachings to help him make this decision?

Finally it hit him. He had surely wandered into a forest of barber's chairs all right, but what was the best way to cut them down? Cut the worst trees out one at a time and leave the strong ones until last. That way you reduce your chance of injury. "Okay," he thought, "What scares me the most here?" He knew that with two small children and a big mortgage, the biggest fear he had was a large, long-term debt. He didn't want to risk his home and the comfort of his family for his job. Also, if he paid his Dad over a long period of time, would his Dad become impatient at some point and want an early settlement? Or if he borrowed from the bank, what would happen if he got behind on the loan? He could lose everything. What were the positive options? If he simply sold the business and went to work for someone else, there would be no debt and he would still have a job. The buyer would have to pay him for his shares too, so he would have some extra money in the bank to support his family. Best of all, he would be working for a big team again, just like he was when he was in the logging camp. He always liked the crew and he liked all of the guys he worked with. He was a team player and he did not relish the idea of being on his own without a big group to support him. His decision was made. He would announce it to Dale tomorrow.

Later that night he told Lydia the whole story. She was supportive of his decision as usual and told him that she would always be there for him. Theirs was a relationship of unconditional love. Lydia had signed on with Walter for the long term and would not let any business issue, no matter how large or small get in the way of their marriage.

The next morning, Walter strode into the offices of Kennedy Insurance Services with a conviction that he had never felt before. He was about to make a major business decision and he expected a lecture from his Dad. The lecture never came.

As he approached Dale's office door, his heart was pounding and his palms were sweating. Nevertheless, he tried to look calm. "Hi Dad," he said.

"Good morning, Walter," came the reply from Dale. "Have you made any decisions?"

"Yes I have, Dad. I want to sell the business to a large company and go to work for them," he said strongly.

"Okay then, Walter. How do you plan to go about that?" asked Dale.

"Jeez Dad, I haven't thought that far ahead. Don't you have someone in mind?"

Walter asked.

Dale seldom left anything to chance and had already done some research. "Well as a matter of fact, the Shelton Saunderson Group is looking for acquisitions. I understand that they want smaller firms with talented young people to help them with their succession plans. Why don't you give them a call? If they show any interest, let me know how it works out." With that he picked up the phone and called his favorite client to set up a golf game. Dale knew that Walter needed to make this deal on his own. He also had full confidence that he would rise to the occasion and do what was right for both of them.

Walter knew about Shelton Saunderson. They were an international insurance brokerage firm with about 175 offices all over North America. They were a force to be reckoned with and had a huge hold on a lot of major National accounts. He wondered if they would actually be interested in purchasing a small office in Northern Ontario. It seemed like unusual strategy for them. Walter leafed through his insurance directory and found the phone number of Craig Ferguson, the regional Vice President of Shelton Saunderson. He had been introduced to Craig at an Insurance Broker's convention some years earlier and hoped he would remember him. As he picked up the phone, he straightened in his chair, cleared his throat and took a deep breath. "Hello Craig, this is Walter Kennedy of Kennedy Insurance Services here," he said in his most professional voice.

"Well Hello to you too, Walter. It's nice to hear from you. We met at that Broker's convention in Toronto about three years ago, didn't we?"

Walter was relieved that Craig remembered him. "Yes, that's right and you gave a great speech about risk analysis and selection, as I recall it."

"And you remembered it?" Craig asked. "You must be the only one there who even remembers that I was on the agenda."

Walter laughed and said, "Well, we had some loss ratio problems and I needed all the help I could get at the time. Your presentation actually helped me out quite a bit."

"Well you're a Heck of diplomat if nothing else, Walter. So what can I do for you today?" Craig asked warmly.

Walter told him the purpose of his call, unaware that Craig Ferguson knew a lot more about Walter Kennedy than he was letting on. Craig's personnel people had been scouting likely young candidates for future management positions and Walter's name had come up on several occasions. They had contacted a placement agency to give him a call two years ago and Walter turned them down flat. Having Walter coming directly to him now was a gift he had not dreamed of. Craig indicated that yes, they were interested in acquisitions. They were planning to expand into rural areas in a big way and were looking for profitable small agencies that they could pick up for cash. Their overall strategy was to become a household name throughout the country by opening up wherever it made financial sense. That would give them increased market share and access to numerous new opportunities. They felt that the international strengths of Shelton Saunderson would nicely compliment the credibility of small but solid local agencies. If the prospective firm had a strong balance sheet and could project a positive five-year return on investment, they wanted to buy it. Along with strong financials, they wanted to see good young employees with advancement and transfer potential. Shelton Saunderson was a firm on the move and they needed knowledgeable, talented young people waiting in the wings in order to assure that they would have long-term succession viability as their older managers retired. Walter was perfect for them and Kennedy Insurance Services was a good fit. Craig asked Walter if he could fly up to Spruce River and see him next week. Walter wasted no time agreeing to the meeting.

Walter could hardly believe what he was hearing. He had made one call and already he had a Senior Vice President of one of the largest firms on the continent coming to discuss an acquisition deal.

When he told his Dad about the call later that day all Dale said was, "Just make sure they don't shaft me son. I want a fair price and I want all of my money up front from these guys. If you can't get that, then I won't sign off on it." Walter knew that Dale meant business and he resolved at that moment to make certain Craig Ferguson did not take advantage of him. He had to be strong and he had to think like a businessman. In his mind he was ready.

On the morning of Craig's visit, Walter shaved twice before putting on his best suit and tie. He looked sharp and he knew it. Lydia was nervous for him and she gave him an extra-long hug as he went out the door. "Just remember that you're my special guy, Walter and you can do anything you want to," she whispered. That made Walter feel a little better, but he still had a knot in his stomach and a tremor in his voice.

"Thanks Honey," he mumbled.

Craig Ferguson turned out to be a first class gentleman. He was an attractive man in his early fifties with a natural aura of confidence and success about him. He was well dressed, well groomed and stood about six feet tall. Nora would comment later that if she weren't already happily married, she would have, "put the moves on him." After he had coffee and some small talk with Walter, Craig made a special point of asking to be introduced to Dale. He knew that this was a family business and that the sale would be a family affair. Insulting the veteran owner would not be wise. Dale was gracious and positive during their discussion. He pointed out that this was Walter's deal, but that he would offer any assistance that they might need of him. He then excused himself on the guise of going to an appointment. Actually, he was having mixed feelings about the sale and wanted to get out of the office to clear his head.

When Craig and Walter finally agreed to get down to the business at hand, Craig started by laying out the basic plan. "Firstly Walter, we will have to bring our comptroller in to do a due-diligence exercise on you books. That is standard procedure, so that we can convince our Board that this is a good deal and that we haven't missed any skeletons that might be rattling around in your closet. Assuming that goes well, we will make an offer based on two hundred percent of your annual commission revenues at the time of ownership transfer. We will not put in any holdback clauses and we will not purchase the non-insurance obligations of the limited corporation. We are only buying the assets of the insurance firm here, so you and your Dad will have to clear up your other business obligations. We will hire all existing staff at their existing compensation, and we will require that you stay on as the manager. You will of course, have to sign an employment contract which will include our standard non-competition agreement. How does it all sound so far?" Walter indicated that it sounded all right and that he wanted to hear more. Craig carried on for another 30 minutes.

Throughout Craig's presentation, Walter mostly just nodded and grunted. "Uh Huh; Okay; and I see," were his only contributions to the discussion. Finally when it was his turn to speak, his thoughts turned to Dale, "Well Craig, I will have to get my Dad's opinion on all of this. Can I see it in writing?"

"Absolutely! When I get back to my office, I will have it drawn up in contract form and send it up to you on overnight courier so that you and Dale can read it over together. After that, I will come back again, and we can get down to work," Craig responded. With that they agreed to end the discussion and walked to Walter's favorite restaurant for lunch.

Walter didn't have much of an appetite and spent

most of the time pushing his food around on the plate. Craig sensed his discomfort. "Look Walter, the main reason we are looking at your firm is because we want to hire *you*. There are hundreds of small agencies in this country that we could purchase, but we have done our homework, and we see you as one of our next senior executives. You are our man and unless I miss my bet, you have a great future with our Company."

Walter looked Craig squarely in the eye and responded, "Thanks Craig, that's very flattering, but it still depends on my Dad. I can't make this decision on my own."

"I understand, Walter. Talk it over with Dale and let me have your decision as soon as you can. If you don't want to do a deal with us, we have some other irons in the fire." Craig offered without flinching.

Walter felt that the deal might be slipping away, and quickly responded, "I don't think it will be a problem."

Walter was right. It wasn't a problem. When the written deal arrived, Dale took it to his lawyers and they advised him to take it. He signed off on it immediately. The corporate comptroller from Shelton Saunderson was happy with the Kennedy Insurance Services records and the state of their financial affairs. The deal was completed in record time and within a month Dale and Martha were kissing Walter, Lydia, and their grandchildren goodbye as they headed out on the road for an extended vacation in their new motorhome. Walter had never seen his parents look so happy. As Dale and Martha's big, shiny Winnebago backed out of the driveway, Walter knew that a new chapter of his life was about to begin.

Chapter 3

Shelton Saunderson

Walter loved working for Shelton Saunderson. Immediately after they took over, they did a full operational review of his office and determined that in order to increase sales and profitability they would have to increase the size of the sales staff. Craig Ferguson had asked his personnel department to find two aggressive young account managers to move into the new operation. Jake Parfeniuk and Ed Hartford were chosen to head up the sales effort under Walter's tutelage. Jake had a lot of experience in head office, but he loved the outdoors. Craig felt that he would fit in well in a smaller community. Ed needed more experience, and moving him there was Craig's opportunity to find out if Walter would be able to handle the training side of his new management position.

ALWAYS REMEMBER: IF IT AIN'T FUN, IT AIN'T WORTH DOING

Both new salesmen fit in right away. They got along well with Walter, Nora and the other staff, and they fit well in the community. They both felt that they had come into a great opportunity. They respected Walter and admired his reputation in Spruce River. Before long they were involved in all kinds of community activities and began moving large amounts of volume into the old Kennedy Insurance portfolio. Jake was able to make a lot of contacts through the Rod and Gun Club and as a long-term member of Rotary, he became a fixture in the community in no time. Ed became Walter's protégé and quickly began forming relationships with the old "Kennedy" clients.

The firm's operating name was changed to *Shelton Saunderson Inc. formerly Kennedy Insurance.* Walter felt a twinge of remorse when the new signs went up, but before long the name felt right to him. He was happy with his position as the local Shelton Saunderson manager and he enjoyed reporting to Craig Ferguson. Craig was always supportive and in no time, he and Walter became allies and good friends.

Over the next two years, more support staff were added as the office volume grew. At the end of the third year, the Kennedy office was producing the highest profit margin in the region. The staff count had risen to fifteen and the Kennedy name was dropped from the signage. Walter was acknowledged not only as a successful Shelton Saunderson manager, but as a great boss. He was known to be a fair man who had the respect of his entire team. His reputation in the Company was excellent and Craig felt that it was time to move him up the ladder.

The current regional head office manager, Bob Jones was ready to retire and they needed a strong young manager to replace him. Head office revenues had been lagging behind the regional average for a few years and he knew that some changes had to be made to satisfy the Board of Directors. Craig could have simply promoted one of his head office unit leaders but he felt that bringing new blood into the top job might just be the injection of energy that they needed.

Craig called Walter and asked him point-blank if he would like to move to Toronto. "Is this a joke Craig?" Walter asked.

"No joke, Walter. Jonsey wants to retire and I want you to replace him," Craig responded.

"Wow, that's quite an offer. Do you think I can handle it?" Walter asked.

"If I didn't, I wouldn't be calling, now would I Walter? I know that this is a big change and that you will want to discuss it with Lydia. Before you do that, let me assure you that your compensation package will be significantly increased, and we will pay all of your moving costs. We want you here Buddy, and I'm not taking no for an answer," Craig stated with conviction. Walter agreed to discuss it with Lydia and get back to Craig the next day.

Walter's mind was reeling. He had been to head office several times and frankly, he found it a bit cold and intimidating. It had a staff of over 100 people and other than the marketing and personnel staff that had helped him out from time to time, the only person he really knew there was Craig Ferguson. How could he hope to take on such a huge position at such an early stage in his career? He was only thirty two years old and he had only managed fifteen people in the past. He consoled himself with the fact that Craig would be there to back him up, but he still felt that he might not be experienced enough for the job. At the same time, he relished the challenge and the status that a head office management job would bring.

Lydia was as supportive as ever. "Walter, if this is good for you, then it is good for the kids and me. If this is what you really want, then let's do it. It will be great fun," she said exuberantly.

"Have I ever told you how much I love you?" Walter asked softly.

"All the time," she crooned. With that, the decision was made.

* * *

Shelton Saunderson decided to move Nora into the management spot at the Kennedy office with Jake Parfeniuk moving up to the assistant manager's position. They felt that Jake's natural affinity for the community along with Nora's knowledge and reputation in the firm would allow for a seamless transition. Walter had recommended that course of action and although he felt some concern for the future of his old office, he was more concerned about his own future. "Nora will do fine," he thought. He was right. The office did very well without him after his move to Toronto.

Walter, Lydia and the kids moved into a nice four-bedroom ranch style house in the High Park area of Toronto. There was a school nearby and the park was handy for the kids to play in. Lydia was very happy and looked forward to getting the kids settled in school and making new friends. Walter had taken a three-week leave of absence in order to get everything moved in, so he had not actually reported for work yet. As he was putting his favorite books onto the shelves in his new den, he was imagining what his new job might be like. His mind's eye had created and reviewed hundreds of scenarios over the past few weeks but he had no idea what he was about to walk into.

Chapter 4

Management Chaos

When Walter walked into his new office for the first time he felt like he was on top of the world. Here he was...a thirty two-year-old insurance man from a small town taking on the largest insurance brokerage office in the country. "Life doesn't get any better than this," he thought.

His office was on the twenty third floor of a newer downtown office building with a view of the waterfront. He had arrived early that morning and wandered around virtually unnoticed until he found his name already mounted in gold lettering on the door of his new office. It was a space suitable for a king, with a huge desk, a sitting area with plush leather bound chairs and a heavy glass topped coffee table. The walls were covered in dark mahogany and large tropical plants were placed strategically about the space. The paintings that adorned the walls were by well-known artists and a closer inspection revealed that they were originals. In the corner opposite the desk was a salt-water aquarium stocked with dozens of large, colorful tropical fish. His chair was a large, classic leather executive wingback tilter that was as comfortable as any chair Walter had ever sat in. The room was massive compared to the office he had in Spruce River. "Jeez you could have a dance in here," Walter whispered to himself. At that moment Craig Ferguson walked in.

"So what do you think of your new digs, Buddy?" Craig asked, holding out his hand.

Walter grabbed Craig's hand and gave it a hearty shake. "Man, you never told me it was going to be like this," He said with a smile.

"This is just an office. It's not the room that will make you successful. It's what you do in it," Craig said challengingly. Walter knew what Craig was getting at, but he still didn't know what lay ahead.

Craig introduced Walter to Karla Petersen whose desk was immediately outside of Walter's office door. She was to be his new assistant. Karla was an attractive woman in her early thirties with a ready smile and an air of confidence. "It's very nice to meet you Karla. I look forward to working with you," Walter said genuinely.

"That's what you say now," she responded with a grin. Although Walter assumed that her smile was an indication that she was joking, he sensed that there was a deeper meaning to her comment. He glanced at Craig who had turned away and was looking around the office with a definite frown.

"Something wrong, Craig?" Walter asked.

"Oh no, just thinking," Craig muttered. "Let me introduce you to Jonesy. He will fill you in on what your job is and what problems he might be leaving for you." Walter was beginning to think that there was more going on here than Craig was telling him.

Bob Jones was a portly, gray haired man in his early sixties. His complexion was quite ruddy from years of heavy drinking and he had a package of cigarettes bulging out of his shirt pocket. After the obligatory handshake, Jonesy said, "So you're the new guy eh? You seem pretty young for this job. How old are you anyway?"

When Walter told him that he was thirty-two, Jonesy laughed so hard that he went into a coughing fit. His face went red and it looked like he might explode. Walter moved toward him in an effort to assist, but Jonesy waved him off saying, "I'll be all right. I've been smoking for almost 50 years and this is God's punishment." When the coughing subsided, Jonesy had tears streaming down his face. He wiped them away with a rumpled handkerchief that he kept wadded up in his back pocket. Finally he spoke, "Well you might be young, but I am damned glad to have you here. I've had it with this job."

Bob Jones noticed that Walter had a strained look of concern on his face after his last comment and felt that he should console him. "Look, I come across a little brash. That's just my way. This is a great company and I am sure you will do well here if you give it a chance. I have been here for thirty years, and its time I moved on. I don't think I have what it takes to manage 147 monkeys anymore," he said with a scowl.

"Monkeys?" Walter asked.

"Well that's what I call them," Jonesy said sheepishly. "You have to keep a firm hand on this bunch. They don't listen and management doesn't have any authority anymore. All we do is worry about lawsuits and employee's rights. Rights? In my day the only right anyone had was the right to get a paycheck. Now they want management to kow-tow to them and when we don't, they go running to the personnel department to get us into trouble. It's all yours Walter. I have had enough. Thank God this is my last week!"

Jonesy excused himself, saying that he had some things to clear up. As he watched Bob Jones walk out of the office, Walter felt like he wanted to run away. What had he gotten himself into here and how was he going to make it work?

The office was in worse shape than Walter thought. After reviewing the organizational chart and the last twelve months of financial results, he knew what he had to do. The office was top heavy on salaries and new sales production was marginal. Operating expenses were not too bad given the size of the office, but the overall revenue did not justify the cost of the operation. He had to maximize profitability by increasing sales production while keeping salaries and expenses in line. He may have to consider reducing the staff count in the short term until revenues could justify additional support. He must review the overall staffing situation as well, as it seemed that there were an inordinate number of people in middle management and support roles and not enough in production. Despite the obvious challenges, managing it would not be much different than his old Kennedy operation, he thought. There were more people and the numbers were larger, but the concepts were the same. He knew that he had to make some changes right away in order to move the office to an acceptable profit margin. If he didn't, the Board might soon be reviewing Craig's decision to hire him.

The next day, when Walter heard Karla settling in at her desk, he yelled out for her to come into his office. Karla got up from her desk and leaned against Walter's doorjamb looking directly at him. "How long have you worked here?" he asked.

"Almost 12 years now," she responded.

"And with all of that experience, what do you think of the place?" he pried.

Karla thought about her response for a moment before answering, "Walter, there are real problems here. You may have bitten off more than you can chew. You have a lot of unhappy people in this office, and frankly, a lot of them are ready to mutiny." Walter pondered that for a moment, while gazing at his fish tank.

"So Karla, why do they want to mutiny? What are the problems that have made them so unhappy?" he asked.

"It's the management," she said. "They don't care about us and they treat us like second class citizens. When we complain, they either ignore us or fire us. Nothing ever changes, and nothing ever will." Walter could see that Karla was quite upset and asked her to sit down. She moved to one of his plush chairs in the sitting area and sat down without saying a word. He got up from his desk and sat in the chair next to her.

Walter, feeling the need to speak, offered, "I hear you Karla. I had a meeting with Bob Jones yesterday and I can see that his management attitudes probably did not keep pace with the new millennium. I, on the other hand...."

Karla interrupted him, saying, "Look Walter, Bob is not the only problem. He is just a pawn in the hands of the Board. He manages the way they want him too. They don't care about us. You can't change that." Her tone was strained and tears were welling up in her eyes.

"Okay Karla. I get it," Walter said calmly. He knew that he had just scratched the surface of the problems at Shelton Saunderson and he knew that he had to do *something*, and soon.

For the rest of the day, Walter wandered around the office visiting with various staff members. He introduced himself to many of them, and asked what their jobs were. He was attempting to find out how they felt about Shelton Saunderson. He observed staff interactions with clients and eavesdropped on coffee-room conversations. He was attempting to be a fly on the wall, but his presence was painfully obvious to all he encountered.

The response Walter got from his new staff was cold and discomforting. They responded with one-word answers and offered nothing in the way of friendliness or support. They would look straight ahead and not make eye contact until he stood in front of their desks and spoke directly to them. They were like zombies. He noticed that their attitudes toward customers were similar. They seldom smiled during client discussions and they kept their conversations short. Customers seldom left the office with a smile on their faces and there were virtually no exchanges of jocularity.

This was so unlike Kennedy Insurance that Walter felt like he had landed in a parallel universe where simple fun and enjoyment had been outlawed. Discussions he overheard offered little in the way of enlightenment, as conversations were kept to a whisper and generally ended completely whenever Walter drew near. Most of the comments he did overhear involved negative commentary about co-workers and complaints about clients. Walter was now convinced that this office had serious problems. The atmosphere at Shelton Saunderson was like nothing he had ever experienced before and it had to change. He spent the next month observing this consistently stilted behavior until one day he decided that he must be more proactive in approaching the problems there.

In an effort to improve communication, Walter called a meeting of the entire staff. The boardroom in the office wasn't large enough for all of them, so he had Karla rent a meeting hall in the Hotel down the street from the office. His message was to be simple. He would tell them that he was the new kid on the block and that he intended to make some changes. The office results were poor and morale was low. He would be restructuring, and at the end of it he expected better results and improved morale. This all made sense to Walter when he had scribbled his thoughts down on paper the night before. What he hadn't counted on was the reaction of the staff.

Walter had been a member of the *Toastmasters* club back in Spruce River, so he knew how to give a speech and was reasonably comfortable as he moved to the lectern and began speaking into the microphone. After introducing himself with a brief history of his career, he opened by showing the last 12 month financial results from the most recent corporate brochure on the overhead screen. He reviewed the year-to-date statistics line by line and explained how each revenue and expense figure impacted on the bottom line. He compared this year's results with last year's results and commented on the reduction in revenue and profitability. He was thankful that he had taken that accounting course at night school while he was working for his father. The financial information made no impact at all on his audience despite his spirited delivery. As he looked out into the room, all he saw was blank stares and bored expressions. He realized that most of these people had no interest in page after page of statistical information, so he decided to change his approach.

Walter cleared his throat and lowered his voice, "Okay people let's be clear on something. I am not here to make your lives worse. I am here to make them better. I don't want to get rid of anyone, and I don't want to make your jobs harder. My Dad had an expression that he always lived by, *'If it ain't fun, it ain't worth doing.'* I want to see happy, smiling faces when I walk around our office and I want you to talk to me about your problems. I can assure you that I won't ignore you, and I won't fire you for being honest. This is a new day and a new opportunity for all of us." He stopped and briefly scanned the audience. When his eyes moved to Karla in the front row, he could see a smile beginning to curl at edges of her mouth.

Heads began to turn as various people in the audience began whispering amongst themselves. "Was this guy for real?" they were muttering. "Does he really expect to make changes that will improve Shelton Saunderson? He's either nuts, or the real thing."

Craig Ferguson was standing at the back of the room with Bob Jones. They too were whispering. When Craig realized that Walter was looking directly at him, he gave him a supportive nod and followed it with a smile. He then turned and left the hall. Jonesy, wanting to hear more took a seat near the door.

Walter started again, "I know that you have been unhappy with the way management has treated you. If that's not the case, then correct me now." He paused and scanned the room again.

No one spoke so he continued, "Okay, so we know that we have a problem. I can't fix what I don't know, so I am going to have to ask for your help. Beginning next Monday, I will be personally interviewing a cross section of our staff. My office door will be closed and your comments will be confidential. If you are open and honest with me, I can effect some good changes. If you are not, things will probably stay the way they are." He paused again. A murmur began to emerge as staff members began whispering amongst themselves again. Walter knew instinctively what the problem was and spoke into the microphone again.

"Look people! This is not a witch-hunt!" he began. "This is an effort to improve things. I am a man of my word and when I tell you that these meetings will be confidential and that your comments will not be held against you, I mean it." With that Walter stopped speaking while collecting his thoughts.

Suddenly a voice came out of the crowd, "Yah, we have heard it all before, Mr. Kennedy. We know what happens in that office of yours. So many people got fired in there that Jonesy refused to move into it when they made him the manager!" As suddenly as the tirade began, it ended and Walter was at a loss as to who had spoken.

Walter reassured the group again that his intentions were good but seeing that he wasn't making any headway, he thanked them all for attending and adjourned the meeting. As his team filed out of the meeting hall, the murmur grew to a dull roar. Walter knew he had a tiger by the tail, and he didn't know if he should tackle it or let it go. He would not sleep well that night.

When Walter got back to his office Jonesy stuck his head though the door and said, "Good speech kid. *'If ain't fun it, it ain't worth doing'*...I love that." Then Bob Jones chuckled, turned on his heel, and wandered off down the hall whistling as he went. It was painfully clear that the happiest person in the office was the one man who only had a few days left to work.

Walter spent the next few days interviewing the staff as promised. Some of the interviews lasted two or three hours while some lasted under half an hour. Some people were very vocal about their concerns and others held back, refusing to say anything that might be held against them. The vocal people gave Walter some insight into the inner workings of Shelton Saunderson but none of them were clear on why they felt the way they did. The office was riddled with fear, anger, suspicion and resentment. Walter would later learn that the emotions of most staff members stemmed from years of favoritism, elitism, sexism, distrust, and a failure to delegate authority. Management had locked up all of the perks and authority in the executive vault and swallowed the key. Most staff members were kept in the dark on important decisions and promotions were reserved for members of the old-boy's network. No one really knew what it took to become a member of the old-boy's network but most of the Shelton Saunderson staff assumed that Walter was a charter member. How could they trust a man who was known to be a friend of the Regional Vice President who was pulled out of a small office in Spruce River, Ontario to manage an office of this magnitude? He must be one of *them*.

A couple of weeks after the ill fated staff meeting, Craig Ferguson sauntered into Walter's office. "Hey buddy, how's it going?" he chirped.

"Well Craig, let me tell you. I have certainly had better days. I just can't seem to get a handle on what exactly is bothering the group here. There is an overwhelming feeling of uneasiness throughout the office, but there seems to be no specific reason for it," Walter responded.

"Well, that's why you get the big bucks. You have the rest of the day to figure it out and fix it," Craig said jokingly. "Let me buy you a cup of coffee," he offered, placing his hand on Walter's shoulder as he walked him through the doorway. As the two men walked down the hallway toward the lunchroom, Walter noticed that various staff members were watching them and whispering amongst themselves again.

Craig, also aware of the whispering muttered, "Rude bunch aren't they? If they have something to say, why don't they just say it?" Walter knew that there was a definite barrier between management and staff in this office and he had to find a way to tear it down.

As Walter drove home that night, looking forward to a weekend off, his mind was full of thoughts about the office. He couldn't stop thinking about the attitude of the Shelton Saunderson staff and what he might be able to do to repair the damage.

He spent the weekend exploring Toronto with Lydia and the kids. He loved the City and he could see that his family was very happy there. Even though it would have been easier to simply pack up and move home to Spruce River, he sensed that this was going to be their home for a long time to come.

As the Kennedy family was driving home from a Bluejays baseball game at Skydome stadium on Sunday evening, Walter ran over a nail on the road. The unmistakable hiss and *whump, whump* sound that followed let him know that he had a flat tire. After years of driving over logging roads, Walter was no stranger to flat tires so he pulled over to the side of the road and set about removing the jack and the spare tire from the car. In no time he had the tire changed and they were on the road home again.

On Monday morning Walter called Karla to let her know that he would be late for work and then he drove over to a tire dealer that he passed on his way to the office every day. The tire needed repairing and he thought he might as well get a wheel alignment while he was there. The car had a vibration at high speeds that had been bothering him for some time.

As Walter pulled his car into Joshua's Tire Center he was drowning in a sea of thoughts. Having a flat tire was a welcome respite for him as it gave him a reason to get to the office a little later than usual. Little did he know that his choice of tire stores would forever change his life.

Chapter 5

Joshua's Tire Center

When Walter walked through the heavy glass doors of Joshua's Tire Center he was immediately impressed with how clean the place was. The floor tiles gleamed and the tires on display were clean and shiny black. The sales counter was tidy and there wasn't a hint of dust or grease anywhere. He knew right away that this was no ordinary tire store.

As he approached the counter, all three clerks looked up, smiled and almost in unison, said good morning to him. As if they had rehearsed their roles, the two women and one man all looked at each other and a young lady with *"Karen"* embroidered on her bright red shirt said, "Can I help you today?" She had a beautiful smile and it was easy to see that she was genuinely enjoying her work.

Walter stepped toward Karen and pointed out the window to his car. He then let her know that he had a flat tire and that he might need a wheel alignment. "No problem sir, I will have one of the guys from the back come out and move your car into the bay. May I have your keys please?" Walter pulled his keys from his pocket and watched her disappear into the back of the shop. He then saw her accompany a well-groomed young man in overalls to his car. She placed a plastic cover over the driver's seat and a paper mat on the floor and then the young man got in and drove the car toward the back of the building, disappearing into an empty bay.

Karen soon re-entered the customer waiting area of the store and walked directly over to Walter. At this point he had assumed a position in one of the clean, comfortable client chairs while leafing through that morning's *Globe and Mail*. He was impressed that this tire shop had three current copies of several major local and National newspapers available for clients. "It shouldn't be too long sir. Would you like a coffee while you wait?" Karen asked with a smile.

"That's sounds great. Let me get it myself," Walter responded.

"That's okay sir. I'll get if for you. How do you take it?" she asked.

Karen reached into a cabinet over the coffee machine and pulled out one of the dozens of identical cups that were stacked neatly inside. Walter asked her for two sugars and a small amount of cream and then watched as she meticulously poured and mixed his coffee in the spotlessly clean red ceramic cup that had *"Joshua's Tire Center"* printed on it in gold leaf. He was impressed that there were no Styrofoam cups in this shop. He imagined that it must be quite costly and time consuming, to have all of those monogrammed cups made and then washed every day. "This is the nicest tire shop I have ever been in," he thought. He also thought it strange that at no point had Karen asked him how he intended to pay for the work he had ordered.

As Walter read the paper and sipped his coffee, the counter clerks worked quietly taking calls, handling clients, and punching away at their computers. They joked and laughed quietly amongst themselves, but at all times, they portrayed a professional, disciplined image. As he viewed the scene before him, he noticed that the clerks never asked for personal information or payment from any of the clients until the work was done. It was as if they had complete trust in every client that chose to enter their shop. "Everything they do here is client oriented and everyone that works here really seems to enjoy their job," he thought as he put his paper down and watched the scene before him. "I wish I could get this kind of morale going in my office," he muttered quietly to himself.

After an hour had passed, Karen came over to Walter again and told him that they had found an unexpected problem with his car. They were concerned that the ball joints in the steering mechanism may be worn and should be replaced. "This is a safety issue, sir and it is extremely important that we bring it to your attention. Our owner will be out shortly to show you the problem," Karen said professionally.

"The owner?" thought Walter. "The owner wants to show me my worn out ball joints. What kind of wondrous place is this?"

Just as Karen was finishing her discussion with Walter a short, balding man in his late fifties, dressed in a bright red shirt and clean khaki pants approached them. Walter could see immediately that this fellow was in good shape. He was thin with no hint of excess weight on any part of his body. He had a healthy glow to his skin and his bright blue eyes sparkled like the ocean on a sunny day. "Hi, I'm Joshua," said the man with his hand outstretched. Walter instinctively stood up, grasped the man's hand and shook it. The handshake was firm but gentle. Joshua wasn't one of those people who tried to impress others with how strong his grip was. A handshake was a gesture of respect to him, not a strongman competition. Walter appreciated that, as he had come across so many men in his life that seemed to want to squeeze the blood out of his fingers whenever they shook his hand. Walter introduced himself to Joshua. At that point Karen excused herself, heading back to her post at the front counter.

Joshua explained the ball joint problem to Walter again. He then invited Walter to come out into the shop with him so that he could show him exactly what was wrong. Walter explained that he had to trust Joshua and if he needed new ball joints, they should replace them right away. He also mentioned that the ball joints were probably responsible for the high speed vibration that he had been experiencing.

Joshua listened to Walter and then said, "I appreciate that you trust me Walter, but it is my policy to make certain that you know what is going on before I do any work that you have not specifically ordered. Humor me. You might find it interesting."

ALWAYS REMEMBER: IF IT AIN'T FUN, IT AIN'T WORTH DOING

Walter followed Joshua out into the shop. His car was on the hoist in the clean, tidy shop, and the same young man that had moved it into the bay was waiting for them under it. Joshua asked the young man to pass him a work light and he pointed up into the bowels of the steering mechanism, showing Walter the leaking ball joint seals. "That leaking tells me that those joints have been running without any lubrication, Walter. That probably means that they are seriously worn, and could give out on you at any moment. You don't have to have them done now, but I sure don't want to see you drive out of here and end up getting into an accident that we could have avoided with a hundred bucks worth of repairs today."

Walter knew a little about cars and agreed that this was a problem that needed attention. He asked Joshua to go ahead and do the work and thanked him for bringing it to his attention. Joshua turned back to the young man, patted him on the back said, "Good catch, Kenny. A lot of lesser mechanics would have missed that problem."

"Thanks Josh," Kenny said softly.

Joshua turned to Walter and said, loud enough for Kenny to hear, "Kenny is one of our best men. You're in good hands with him." Kenny smiled confidently but Walter noticed he was blushing as he went back to his work.

"Well Walter, it looks like you are going to be here for a little while longer. How about we grab a cup of coffee and go into my office?" Joshua asked. Walter took him up on his offer without hesitation. He was interested in Joshua and the way he did business. He could see that everyone at Joshua's Tire Center enjoyed their work and more importantly, they liked working for Joshua. He also knew that he had not been taken advantage of. Joshua made sure of that. This was a very special business and Walter had to learn more.

When they sat down in Joshua's clean but Spartan office Walter noticed that there were a lot of group photographs and some individual photos of various men and women on the wall. "So who are all of these people on the walls, Josh?" he asked.

"Well, on this wall behind me, you have the photos of the staff in this branch. On that wall and that wall, I've got photos of the staff in my other 35 branches. And over here, I have individual photos of the folks that once worked for me that have since passed away. Fortunately there are only 4 of those," said Josh.

Walter was impressed. This unassuming man had thirty-six Joshua's Tire Center branches. "Wow, I had no idea that your Company was so big!" he said.

"Yes, and growing every day. I have another three in the works and I should have them all up and running by the end of the year," Josh announced proudly.

"And what do you do, Walter?" Joshua asked politely. Walter explained that he had recently been transferred from Spruce River as the new branch manager of the Regional Head office of Shelton Saunderson."

Joshua grinned and sat up in his chair, saying, "Guess what Walter? I'm one of your clients. I have been buying the insurance for my little operation from Shelton Saunderson ever since I started it 20 years ago. Is this a small world or what?" Walter was very pleased. Now he had something in common with this intriguing man and he would be more comfortable asking him questions.

"So, who do you deal with over there, Josh?" Walter asked.

"Well, let me see. I started out dealing with Craig Ferguson, until they kicked him upstairs, and then I dealt with a guy named Joe White until they fired him, and then I had Bob Jones until they made him the manager and now frankly I couldn't tell you who I deal with. I get letters from different people all the time. Your company is going through a lot of changes, I guess," Josh said with an inquisitive smile.

Walter was curious as to why this obviously successful businessman would deal with a firm where he didn't even know the name of the person he was dealing with. "Tell me Josh, what makes you keep doing business with us?" he asked.

Josh patiently explained that Shelton Saunderson was there for him when he was starting out. Their firm was smaller then and they had more time for their clients. They looked after him very well and he felt he owed them something. Craig Ferguson was the first insurance broker that he had ever dealt with and as long as Craig was with them, he would probably continue to deal there.

Although Walter was relieved that Joshua's Tire Center was a loyal customer, he was very concerned that this important client was being virtually ignored by the Shelton Saunderson staff. This was yet another problem that he would have to address when he got back to the office. Right now though, he wanted to delve further into Josh's management style.

"So Josh, can I ask you something?" he asked.

"Sure, ask me anything," said Joshua, leaning forward in his chair. Although he didn't know it at the time, Walter was about to begin a dialogue that would set the stage for a new era at Shelton Saunderson.

"What's your secret?" Walter asked, staring into Josh's eyes.

Joshua laughed and answered, "I don't have many secrets Walter."

I'm very impressed with your shop and the staff that work here," Walter stated emphatically. The front end is spotless, and your people are completely professional."

"Well, thanks a lot Walter. We keep trying," Josh responded with a look of obvious pride on his face.

"I have never seen a group of employees who seem so dedicated to client service and to each other. Your people really seem to like each other and they obviously like working here By the way, they like you too. How did you make all of this happen?" Walter asked sincerely.

Although he was flattered by Walter's comments, Joshua could see that the younger man was looking for help. He had taken a shine to Walter and felt that this young man had what it would take to make a difference at Shelton Saunderson. He knew that there were problems there, and at that moment he decided to offer Walter whatever wisdom he might have acquired during his fifty-six years of life.

Chapter 6

Start at the Beginning

"Walter, are you looking for some pointers on how to run Shelton Saunderson?" Joshua O'Hare asked pointedly.

As if he had been waiting for this cue, Walter responded, "You bet I am! I have the unhappiest bunch of people that I have ever seen in my life working for me. They are so miserable in their jobs that just going into the office every day is a struggle. They hate management and they seldom speak to each other. I have talked to a lot of them and I have heard all kinds of vague complaints about how things are, but nothing about how they got that way. No one seems to know why they are unhappy. They just are. Worst of all, this terrible morale problem has affected production and profitability to the point that I may be forced to reduce the staff count. You know from your own experience that service levels have dropped off and because of it we are in danger of losing our hold on existing clients. This is awful. I just don't know where to start trying to fix it all!"

Josh leaned back in his chair, gazing at Walter while clasping his hands behind his head and crossing his legs. Walter slumped back in his chair and waited for Joshua to respond to his tirade. His face had taken on the defeated, yet hopeful look of a small boy who had just admitted to his Dad that he had broken a neighbor's window with his football.

"Have you got any idea what the major problem might be?" Josh began, as he sat forward and placed his hands face down on the surface of his desk. Walter rolled his eyes and looked toward the ceiling without speaking. Sensing that Walter wasn't going to answer, Joshua continued on, "I expect each person will put a different spin on the problems, but if you ask the right questions, eventually a common thread will appear. To find that thread, you must get their trust, and you must show them that you care about their answers."

Now Walter was becoming frustrated. He was mentally reviewing his discussions with the staff, wondering what he could have done better. "Okay Josh, I know that your heart is in the right place, but I really don't know how to find that thread, and I really don't know where to begin looking. How do I get to the point where they trust me?" Walter asked while sitting back in his chair with his hands outstretched in front of him.

"Let's start at the beginning," Josh said with a smile. "You know that the problems in your office began long before you got there. That gives you an advantage. You were not the author of the problems and you have no residual guilt from past transgressions. Shelton Saunderson is an old firm. They have been building their business for over fifty years. Half a century ago management styles were different and I suspect that the Boards of Directors and senior management have never updated their script. I know from my discussions with Craig Ferguson that he has never embraced modern management thinking, and he continues to act like Ebenezer Scrooge and General George Patten all wrapped up in one."

Walter laughed while Josh kept speaking. "This is the new millennium and you cannot allow Shelton Saunderson to continue to treat their staff the way they did in the fifties. In those days, we had just come out of a war effort and money was tight. Anyone who was fortunate enough to have a steady job was happy to have it, no matter how menial it was. Back then, the parents of the workers had lived through the great depression of the thirties and had taught their kids that hard work and compliance with the rules were the only way to survive. There was no time for patience and understanding in the work place because no matter how much production occurred, revenue was small and profits were miniscule. Benefits programs did not exist and workers were only paid for the time they put in. If they were paid on a piecework basis, as they were in a lot of factories, they only got paid for the product they turned out. If they got sick, no one cared. If they didn't show up for work, they were replaced. They simply didn't get paid unless they were there. That environment naturally gave management the upper hand. Workers could be eliminated at the whim of the bosses without so much as a *"how do you do?"* Employers had no need to give reasons for terminations. If they decided that they wanted you gone, they fired you and that was that. Workers had no control over their future and no choice but to do exactly what they were told. That was the environment that created the need for unions and whether you like it or not, those unions have directly and indirectly created the working environment that we have today." Josh took a deep breath, while considering his next comments.

Walter was uncomfortable with the lull in Josh's conversation, and felt the need to speak. "Yes Josh, my Dad gave me a similar lecture when I started working for him. I was just waiting for you to tell me that I have no idea how good I've got it, like he used to," Walter said with a grin.

Josh laughed and said, "Don't tempt me, young fella! I'm sure that I am not as smart as your Dad Walter, but I am sure he would agree with my thoughts on new millennium management," Joshua stated confidently. Walter leaned forward and renewed his focus on Joshua's words. He knew that Josh was about to share some of his thoughts on the current problems at Shelton Saunderson.

"In the old days," Josh said with a smile, "employees had no rights. They were simply tools of management and they were fortunate to have a job. As unions grew, so did other interest groups. As an example, when the women's liberation movement was founded, and began to flourish, management had to take a long, hard look at itself in light of the unpleasant realization that women had been taken advantage of in the work force for far too long. That realization began an entire new way of thinking in management circles and personnel departments all over North America. No longer were we allowed to assume that women could only be receptionists, typists, and cleaning ladies for minimum wages. Managers had to adjust their thinking and begin to provide women with opportunities equivalent to men of equal skill. Women had to be considered for promotions and they had to be allowed the same opportunities for training that men had always enjoyed. The same holds true for ethnic minorities. The old days of obvious racial prejudice are behind us but a secret, hidden race war continues in the minds of many people. I believe we have advanced a long way from the old *sweat shop* days, but I don't think we have fully integrated women and minorities into the upper echelons of many corporations. That will come in time as younger management people like you move up the ladder. However, some corporations still maintain that old style of management. They pretend to provide opportunities for women, when in fact the major decision-makers in their companies are all men. Those men have no intention of letting loose of their hold on the reins of power and they will continue to relegate women to subservient positions and lower pay. I believe that Shelton Saunderson is one of those companies, Walter."

"Well, I don't disagree with what you are saying Josh, but I have interviewed quite a number of people in the office, and not one of them has said anything about male chauvinism or sexual discrimination," Walter interjected.

Josh answered immediately, "I'm not surprised Walter. In an organization where discrimination is rampant, most staff members will simply be afraid to bring the subject up for fear of losing their jobs. If you can gain their respect and if they are confident that you are on their side, they will begin to open up to you. Of course, you must be sincere and you must believe that there is a problem before you can convince them that you want to change things. This may mean that you will have to become critical of current management practices and you will have to work with your superiors to make the changes that you believe in. This will require a lot of intestinal fortitude Walter, and I hope you are up to the task."

Walter didn't reply. He knew that Josh was giving him valuable advice and he decided that his interjections would only reduce his chances of learning what he needed to know. He sensed that Josh knew what he was talking about and he could tell that this man was sincere. As much as he appreciated the advice, he wondered why Josh was spending so much time with him.

Seeing that Walter had nothing to say, Josh continued, "The women's liberation movement led to even greater changes in the workplace. Society began to place greater demands on management. Handicapped people could no longer be rejected for employment or kept in lowly, demeaning jobs. Management found that people with handicaps could in fact fulfill worthwhile positions and make valuable contributions to their organizations. As you know, many organizations now give preferential treatment to handicapped people in an effort to integrate them into the work force. On that subject, I must tell you about a fellow by the name of Chad in my shop that lost an arm in an industrial accident 10 years ago. He thought

ALWAYS REMEMBER: IF IT AIN'T FUN, IT AIN'T WORTH DOING

he was virtually unemployable but I kind of liked him and decided to take him on. When his rehab' councilor called me about him, I really didn't think that he would work out. However, when I met him and saw the look of defeat in his eyes, I wanted to give him a chance. Today, he is one of my most competent mechanics, and it is amazing to watch him work. He has a great sense of humor about his handicap and the other mechanics love working with him. I don't mind telling you that for a lot of reasons, he is one of the best hires I have ever made."

Walter could see small tears welling up in Josh's eyes as he spoke about Chad.

He knew then that this man was sincere.

Aware of Walter's scrutiny, Josh changed the subject. "During the years after the war, production was all that mattered, so people had to produce or they were eliminated. Benefits programs, which would allow them to carry on during an illness or feed their families after an injury or death, were not available. As society began to realize that their people were their strength, corporations were forced to show concern and sympathy for their staff members and treat them like family. This concern has grown to the point where benefits plans are commonplace and instead of eliminating people, we tend to care for them in their time of need. We have established employee assistance programs to help them with everything from depression to legal problems. We help them in much the same manner as we would our own children. However, in some companies these measures are offered grudgingly and often utilization of costly benefits may be the beginning of the end for some employees. Again Walter, I suspect that Shelton

Saunderson may be one of those companies that only pay lip service to their social obligations. Be wary of managers who complain about the cost of benefits programs or who exhibit impatience or disgust with staff members who have genuine problems."

Walter began to recall some of the comments that both Craig Ferguson and Bob Jones had made during his first days in the office. He knew that Josh was acquainted with both of those men and wondered if he was referring to them.

Josh continued, "Now the best employers create extremely safe working conditions in their workplaces and they have genuine concern for all of their staff members. Employees are treated with respect and given every opportunity to advance. Workers *do* have rights now and it is our job as managers to assure that their rights are recognized and maintained. If we could just eliminate all of the bad managers, we could move into the new millennium with our collective corporate heads held high. Your job is to make Shelton Saunderson one of the best employers in the insurance industry. If you believe that you can make the necessary changes in your office to improve the lives of your staff, you will become recognized as an *Employer of Choice* and there will be no stopping you."

Walter smiled at Josh's enthusiasm. He was in awe of this man's sincerity and his knowledge of management matters.

Josh shifted in his chair and his face took on a look of concern as he began speaking again, "The only problem with all of these improvements is that some employees take unfair advantage of them. In all organizations, you

ALWAYS REMEMBER: IF IT AIN'T FUN, IT AIN'T WORTH DOING

will find slackers and people with what I call *toxic personalities*. These people thrive on getting away with things and many of them have an almost pathological need to encourage other employees to be as difficult as they are. They have an exaggerated view of employee rights and they often despise management. These folks will talk trash about you behind your back and when they see another employee getting along with you, they will do everything they can to discredit you. They seem to be generally unhappy in and out of the office, and they have a need to make everyone else as unhappy as they are. Watch out for these people Walter. They are your *Brutus* and you are their *Caesar*. They exist in most organizations and the only thing you can do is ferret them out and minimize the damage that they will try to do. Once you have them pegged you should try to amend their attitude by winning them over. Interestingly, your respect rating will rise with everyone else if you are able to get one of these negative, disengaged people to move over to your side. On the other hand, if you simply cannot get through to them, you may have to eliminate them in order to preserve and maintain the integrity of your team."

Walter was frowning now. This was the first time Josh had said anything negative about staff. Up to this point he had been floating on a cloud of optimism. Now the grim reality of the dark side of management had hit home. He was thinking that everyone at Shelton Saunderson must have a *toxic personality* considering all of the whispering that had been going on behind his back since he arrived.

Josh could see that Walter was worried so he laughed

and said, "Hey Walter don't worry about it. From what I've seen, most of the folks in your office are nice people. With your charm and your winning smile, I am sure you will have them all eating out of your hand in no time."

At that point Kenny stuck his head in the door and said, "Excuse me Josh, but Mr. Kennedy's car is all ready to go. Shall I bring it around front, Mr. Kennedy?"

"Yes and thanks, Kenny." Walter responded while reaching out toward him in an effort to shake his hand.

Kenny smiled and pushed his hand toward Walter. He withdrew it almost immediately, saying, "Sorry, I can't shake your hand Mr. Kennedy. Too much grease on it." Walter and Josh both laughed as Kenny turned and walked toward Walter's car.

"He's a good one," Josh said as if to reconfirm his earlier praise of Kenny.

Looking toward Josh, Walter said laughingly, "Well Josh I have to say that this the most interesting car repair job I have ever had. I'm glad I came in here today. Now if I can just make my office a little like your shop, I might even survive until I get my next flat tire."

"You will Walter, you will. Just remember the old saying, "***If it ain't fun, it ain't worth doing,***" and you will be fine," Josh said while rising to his feet.

"Wow, it's so funny that you would use that expression. My dad used to say that. I used to think it made a lot of sense, but I am beginning to wonder. I'm not having much fun these days," Walter stated in a matter of fact tone.

Josh took Walter's hand and gripped his shoulder saying, "Keep a stiff upper lip, Walter and if you ever need someone to talk to, drop around. I'm usually here."

ALWAYS REMEMBER: IF IT AIN'T FUN, IT AIN'T WORTH DOING

Walter shook Joshua's hand and said that he definitely would be back. As he drove away, Walter was feeling a little inadequate but ever so pleased that he had met Joshua O'hare that morning.

Chapter 7

Earn Your Stripes

Walter considered Josh's advice for several days before acting on it. On the morning when he thought the time was right, he said good morning to Karla and went straight to Craig Ferguson's office. When Walter appeared at his door, Craig smiled and asked him how things were going. "Well Craig, I have been doing a lot of thinking lately, and I have come to the conclusion that we need to make some changes around here," Walter stated with conviction.

"Oh really. And what exactly did you want to change?" Craig asked, wrinkling his forehead and looking over the top of his reading glasses. Walter thought that he might be navigating dangerous waters with Craig now, but decided to forge on. He recalled Josh's comments about old-style management and hoped that Craig would be in agreement with what he was about to say.

Walter took a deep a breath and began speaking, "Craig, my observations so far indicate that we have an unhappy work-force here. Staff members keep telling me that things will never change and that managers like me are just puppets of the Board of Directors. That suggests to me that we have old-style management at the top. I want to move this company into the twenty first century."

Craig, virtually expressionless looked at Walter and said one word, "Really."

Walter sensed the tension in Craig's response but was determined to carry on. "I know that we have a benefits program here and I know that we provide an employee assistance program. I also know that we do not have even one female department manager and I have yet to see a handicapped person on the premises or anyone from an ethnic minority doing anything more than janitorial work. I don't want to cast any aspersions on the integrity of senior management or the Board of Directors, but these things suggest to me that we may be managing this firm like we would have in the fifties. I suspect that the reason people whisper about us behind our backs is because they feel like second class citizens and they resent the fact that managers have incredible perks while they have none. We are on the verge of a major uprising here and we need to get into the trenches and work with the staff to change their view of us."

Before Walter could continue, Craig removed his reading glasses, sat up in his chair and said in a deliberately loud voice, "Well, well, it sounds like you have been reading some new-age management books. It also sounds like you might have forgotten who hired you, who signs your paycheck, and what your job is." Walter knew he was in trouble now. The muscles in Craig's face had tightened and a vein was throbbing in his forehead. At that moment in time Craig looked much older. For the first time since he knew him Walter sensed that his friend was truly angry with him.

In an attempt to diffuse the situation, Walter spoke again, "Look Craig, I don't want to fight with you. I just think that we aren't keeping pace with our competitors in terms of employee satisfaction and it is beginning to cause problems. You were at the meeting I called the other day. Have you ever seen an unhappier group in your life?"

Craig's facial muscles relaxed as he sat back in his chair. He put his hand to his cheek and stared at Walter before speaking. Walter reminded him of himself twenty years earlier so he understood his emotion and he certainly didn't want to lose him. He had seen more than one angry young man walk off the job in his time. Finally he said, "Look Walter, you are new here. I understand that you want to make changes and you want everything done your way. However, this isn't Spruce River and it's not Kennedy Insurance Services. It is in fact Shelton Saunderson and despite your dim view of our management style, we have been highly successful for many years so we must have done something right. What I want you to do is get to know the staff here and improve the bottom line. That is your mandate and you will not accomplish it by beating up on senior management or the Board of Directors. You will do better by *getting into the*

ALWAYS REMEMBER: IF IT AIN'T FUN, IT AIN'T WORTH DOING

trenches as you say, and starting to work with these people. Forget about senior management and the Board and get on with the business of doing business. You have to earn your stripes one at a time before anyone is going to listen to any massive transformation plans." Craig could see that Walter was about to speak again so he pre-empted him by saying, "Do we understand each other?" Walter felt that a hasty retreat would be the best course of action. He apologized for his comments and left Craig's office. Craig smiled to himself as Walter turned and walked away. He was almost smug in his confidence that Walter would do whatever was necessary to improve things and make Shelton Saunderson even greater than it already was.

As Walter drove home that night, his mind was racing. He thought that he had come very close to losing his friendship with Craig, and maybe his job. He understood completely what Craig was saying, but he knew in his heart that changes had to be made. "What should I do?" he thought. As he rounded the corner to his house, he remembered Joshua O'Hare and considered that Josh might be able to help him. He did a U-turn in front of his house and drove back to Joshua's Tire Center.

Josh was just locking the front door of his shop when Walter drove into his parking lot. Recognizing Walter as he made is way to the building, he immediately opened the door and welcomed him in. "Howdy Walter," Josh said, smiling.

"Can I have a minute of your time Josh," Walter asked politely, with barely an expression on his face. Sensing that Walter was carrying a very heavy load, Josh invited him into his office. The two men strode silently through the shop, not looking at each other until they sat down. Walter remained silent until Josh broke the ice.

"Well young man, I gather that something is bothering you. How can I help?" Josh asked.

Walter thought about what he was going to say before he began speaking. "Well Josh, I think I may have blown my credibility at work today, and it is bothering the Heck out of me. I said some things to Craig that I shouldn't have, and I think I may have destroyed our relationship." Josh frowned as he looked at Walter's strained face. He had expected Walter to make some mistakes in his new position, but he didn't expect them to occur so quickly. He felt that he may be responsible for Walter's current situation after his last lecture and wanted to help. Josh knew that listening was more important than speaking at this juncture, so he asked Walter to tell him what had happened.

Walter's voice cracked as he began speaking, "I was pumped when I left here the last time we met, and I wanted to share your ideas with Craig. I marched into his office and laid down the law about how we needed to change the company for the better. It turned out that Craig didn't like my attitude very much. He made it very clear that my opinions were not appreciated and that I should just get on with doing business. He told me that I had to earn my stripes one at a time. I think I offended him and now I am deathly afraid that I might be on the verge of losing my job."

Josh was at a disadvantage as he had not been there to see Craig's facial expressions or his body language. He knew though that Craig was a fair man and it seemed unlikely that one disagreement would mean the end of

ALWAYS REMEMBER: IF IT AIN'T FUN, IT AIN'T WORTH DOING

Walter's career. Nevertheless, Walter had to learn diplomacy and how to present his case without appearing confrontational. He could see that Walter was in a bad spot, so he decided to change his tack and approach the situation from a different perspective. Josh deliberately lowered his voice and spoke softly, "Man oh man, Walter, it sounds like you gave it to him with both barrels. You were right in your thinking of course, but it sounds like you may have been a tad harsh. I think I may have misled you but I really didn't expect you to be so critical right off the bat. No one likes to be told they are wrong and no one likes to be criticized by a new employee. Even though you are a manager, you are still an employee. You will have to follow the company line until you are able to convince the company to consider your way of thinking. Unfortunately, Craig was right. You have to earn your stripes before you start acting like a sergeant. Every private in the army thinks he has a better way of doing things, but no one listens to them until they have been through some battles and earned the right. Try the *nice guy* approach from now on. After all, you can catch a lot more flies with honey than you can with vinegar. I really don't think that Craig is going to fire you over a moment of youthful enthusiasm, but he will be on his guard for a while until he feels comfortable with you again. You have to win him over Walter, because without him, you have no power-base from which to launch your plans. Craig stands between you and the Board of Directors. You must have him on your side so that he can deliver your plans and ideas to them with a conviction of his own. You will have to be diplomatic and you will have to start small. Get one person on your side first, then another, and then another. Trust is contagious and it will spread. Move into each department, showing them that you have their best interests at heart. Plan some new initiatives that will help staff members with their jobs and make them feel that you are genuine in your intentions. In no time at all, Craig and the Board will see the improvements you are making and allow you greater latitude to make your big changes. What you are trying to do will not happen overnight, Walter. It is a long-term project and it will require small steps."

Walter listened intently as Josh spoke to him. He wished he could turn the clock back and do this day over again. He agreed with everything Josh said and only hoped that he could live up to his expectations.

Josh sat back in his chair waiting for Walter to say something. Instead of speaking, Walter scanned the photos of the Joshua's Tire Center's staff on the wall. When his eyes finally met Josh's kindly face, he said, "You know what Josh? I am so glad that I met you. One day, I am going to have photos of my staff on the wall just like these and I hope that my staff will respect me the way yours respect you. Can I call on you from time to time for help? I think I need a seasoned General like you to teach me how to earn my stripes."

Josh laughed as he came around his desk and patted Walter on the shoulder. "Walter, I enjoy talking to you and frankly, I like the way you listen. It's good for my ego, you know. I'm sure that you really don't need me as much as you think, but feel free to drop around any time you want to talk," he said with a wink and a smile. The two men embraced and slapped each other on the back

ALWAYS REMEMBER: IF IT AIN'T FUN, IT AIN'T WORTH DOING

before Walter made his way out of the shop and into his car for the short drive home. Josh knew that Walter had a good heart and that he would fail only if Craig and the Board of Directors did not give him a chance. He would do everything he could to prevent that from happening.

Chapter 8

You Are My Manager...Not My Friend

With Josh's word's ringing in his ears and his ego still smarting from Craig's tongue lashing, Walter went to work the following week with a new sense of direction. He was determined to become a trusted ally to the staff in order to gain their respect. Even though he wanted to have this happen quickly, he knew that Josh was right. He would have to take small steps and work on one person at a time.

He spent a good deal of time reviewing some of the staff interviews that he had already done, looking for signs of common problems. He could see from the comments he found in his notes, that staff members were generally concerned about the lack of communication between managers and employees. That was a common thread. He decided to begin there. He would

ALWAYS REMEMBER: IF IT AIN'T FUN, IT AIN'T WORTH DOING

immediately start to communicate in a very meaningful way. After all, back home in Spruce River, the people in his Dad's office communicated with each other all the time. This he thought, should be a very easy problem to overcome.

Walter decided to confront the staff in their own environment. When lunchtime rolled around, with his plan clear in his mind, he walked down to the staff lunchroom to begin his master plan for improved communication. He thought that he would simply strike up conversations with various people as they ate their lunch. At Kennedy insurance, lunchtime conversations about everything from fishing to automobile repairs and from childbirth to Christmas presents were common. After all, they were all friends there. How could Shelton Saunderson be so different? He was about to find out.

As he drew close to the lunchroom door, he could hear the din of many conversations going on at once. It was a large room with several tables that held up to 70 people at one time. This was a popular gathering spot for many of the staff and even those who were not eating took advantage of the time to catch up on current events with their colleagues. He entered the room with a deliberate air of confidence and a smile on his face. As if a switch had been turned off, the noise in the room abated and conversations stopped. Undeterred, Walter walked to the coffee machine and poured himself a cup of coffee. His assistant Karla, sensing his discomfort left her table and walked over to Walter to engage him in conversation. As she spoke, the noise in the room picked up and the murmur of a myriad of conversations resumed. Walter thought that it was as if Karla's

85

intervention with him had saved the others from a fate worse than death. This was going to be tougher than he had expected.

Karla had quite taken to Walter and knew that he was going to have a hard job getting through to the staff. With a smile on her face she said, "I must say that it is very brave of you to enter the lair of the *great unwashed* at lunchtime, Walter. I don't think that there has been another branch manager in here in decades."

"Well, that's the image that I am trying to overcome, Karla. I want these people to realize that I am one of them, rather than someone to be feared or hated," Walter responded.

"I don't think they hate you yet Walter. They do fear you though!" Karla said with a giggle.

Walter laughed with Karla as he surveyed the room. Still not sure of his next move, he leaned against the counter next to the coffee machine as if his hip had been attached to it with super glue. Some people were ignoring him completely as they munched on sandwiches and chatted with their neighbors. Others would look up and glance nervously his way as they spoke and ate, while still others whispered amongst themselves, occasionally breaking into uproarious laughter as they looked toward him. In his attempt to mingle casually with his team, Walter had become the reluctant center of attention.

Determined to break through, Walter thanked Karla for taking time to talk to him and ventured into the bowels of the lunchroom. As he walked away from her, Karla winked and said, "Good luck!"

He stopped at a table in the middle of the room and took a seat in a solitary empty chair. There were six people seated around the table. As he sat down, they all looked his way with anticipation. No one spoke. Walter expected this reaction and was ready to dole out his small town charm. "Howdy folks, I'm Walter, the new branch manager. Mind if I join you?" He was using his best smile and was summoning up all of the welcoming body language that he could muster. Only the young lady seated directly across from him spoke.

"No problem, Mr. Kennedy," was all she said.

They all concentrated on their lunches as Walter fumbled for words. "So how is everyone?" he asked while scanning the group.

The same girl responded to him again, nervously this time, "I think we're okay Mr. Kennedy. Just having lunch, you know. We all get an hour for lunch."

Walter knew he was getting no where and the tension was beginning to make him sweat. He directed his attention toward the one person who had responded to him, "So what have you got planned for the weekend? By the way, I don't think I caught your name."

"I'm Sarah Jones and this is Dick Yandeau, and Susan Smith next to him, and Barb Johnston, and Carmen Batista, and Laura Yongren is beside you." she said confidently.

"Great. It's nice to finally meet all of you. This place is so big that I am afraid that I just haven't had time to get around to everyone's desk yet," Walter said enthusiastically. Walter's question about Sarah's weekend plans was lost as the six people squirmed with discomfort in their seats. This was a small start, but at least he had one person talking to him. Walter felt that he was truly making headway, *one person at a time*.

Desperate to get beyond introductions, Walter asked Sarah again what she was planning for the weekend. Sarah rolled her eyes upward and responded, "I don't know. I hope you aren't planning to tell me that I have to work overtime this weekend?"

Frustrated, Walter said, "God no Sarah. I'm just interested in the group and I thought that maybe we could chat about ourselves. I have no ulterior motives."

Relieved, Sarah said, "Well, I have no plans. I really can't afford to do much. What are you going to do?"

Without missing a beat, Walter said, "I'm glad you asked. I'm planning to take my wife and kids to Niagara Falls, spend the night in a nice hotel, and go for a ride on the *Maid of the Mist*. I think that should be fun."

Dick Yandeau, sitting next to Sarah mumbled, "It must be nice to have his money."

Not able to hear him clearly, Walter asked, "What was that, Dick?"

"Nothing, nothing," Dick responded. He then got up from the table, and left the room. Dick's leaving seemed to be a secret cue to the others. All but Sarah got up from their chairs silently and left the room. There was no whispering this time. They filed out individually not looking at each other or speaking. Sarah stayed behind to clean the table.

With her hands full of sandwich bags and paper cups Sarah looked at Walter with a smile and said, "Don't worry about them. They're just a bunch of sour pusses." Walter smiled and thanked her for that. He knew that Sarah was trying to be kind. In his mind, that was a big step.

When he returned to his office, Walter stopped at

ALWAYS REMEMBER: IF IT AIN'T FUN, IT AIN'T WORTH DOING

Karla's desk and asked her about Sarah. Karla told him that Sarah was a junior marketing clerk who had been overlooked many times for promotions. Karla felt that even though she was usually forgotten due to her quiet nature, she had a great personality and a work ethic that was second to none. Sarah was a single mother of two children, who had to pay for daycare and could not afford to buy quality clothing. Because she was absent at most company functions, and because she did not dress as well as some of her counterparts, previous management did not think very highly of her, if they knew of her existence at all. Walter was intrigued by Karla's insight into Sarah's situation and her apparent understanding of management's thinking.

"So, is Sarah a friend of yours?" Walter asked.

"Yes she is. But don't think that I am building her up just because of that," Karla answered defensively.

Sensing Karla's displeasure, Walter said, "No, no I didn't mean that. I'm just a little envious that you have friends in this office. I am a little weak in that regard you know."

Karla laughed and said, "You're the manager, Walter. You're not supposed to have friends." Even though Walter knew that Karla was joking, he sensed that there was a certain amount of truth to what she said.

Although his first attempt at making friends in the office had been an unqualified failure, Walter was determined to keep trying. He spent the next several days wandering around the office, chatting with people during coffee breaks. He was still gun-shy from his lunchtime fiasco so he deliberately avoided the lunchroom. He was saving that for a day in the future when he could be comfortable that he would receive a warmer reception.

Walter also spent a good deal of time stopping by various staff members' desks, initiating discussions. He found that although they were warming up to some extent and seemed less unnerved by his presence, they would not open up about their personal lives and would not discuss their specific, work related challenges. After two weeks of trying, he still had no real friends in the office and he still sensed that they were not comfortable with the management of Shelton Saunderson.

He found that his relationships with department managers and supervisors were becoming stronger, but he did not trust the motives of some of them. A few of these people seemed to open up to him only when they needed relief from a corporate directive or wanted to be excused for poor performance. When they weren't looking for a favor, they avoided him like the plague. Those who performed well and toed the corporate line were generally as aloof as they had been when he first arrived.

Walter was becoming overwhelmed with a deep sense of anxiety. His physical well being was suffering and he occasionally felt disoriented and dizzy. He visited his new family doctor who advised that these were common symptoms of distress. They weren't serious at the moment, but he had to eliminate the source of his stress to avoid problems in the future. He wasn't certain what was causing the problem, but he knew that he needed a sounding board outside of the office. He turned again to Joshua O'Hare.

When he walked into Joshua's Tire Centre this time,

Karen and 3 other staff members chimed, "Good Morning Mr. Kennedy," in unison. Walter returned their greeting, all the while feeling a huge twinge of jealousy at the great environment here. "What is Josh feeding these people?" he thought.

Josh greeted him with a smile and a pat on the shoulder. "Want coffee, Walt?" he asked.

"Sure Josh, I'll have coffee and a side order of advice if you don't mind," Walter quipped.

"You got it," said Josh.

When Walter was through explaining his lack of success in making friends of the staff, Josh leaned forward and said, "Jeez Walter, what on earth made you think that you could be their friend. You are the manager aren't you?"

Taken aback, Walter said "But I thought that if I became a personal friend and hung out with them, they would be happier working for me. What did I do wrong?"

"Walter, Walter, Walter," Josh said with a tinge of annoyance, "you need to get their trust all right, but you cannot be their *buddy* and their boss at the same time this early in the game. They know that you make decisions that affect their lives and that you make significantly more money than them. There is no commonality between you that will allow for ordinary friendship. It's not like your old office where you only had a few people who were mainly long term employees. In a workplace the size of Shelton Saunderson, your friendship can only be based in trust and respect. You will have to earn that over time.

Don't expect to be invited to their homes for dinner or

to their children's graduation parties. That might happen eventually, but never assume it. The most you can really expect is that they confide in you when they need your help and that they work hard for you out of simple respect. If they believe that you are fair, that you respect them and that you care about them, they will treat you in a friendly fashion and return your kindness with hard work. Sorry to say Walter, most of them still won't invite you to their kid's graduation parties though." Josh finished speaking with a short laugh.

Walter blushed and replied with a simple, "I get it."

Josh began again, "Just dial it down it a bit. When you talk to them, don't get into personal issues unless they bring them up. Some will want you to be their father confessor, while others will not want you to have any idea about their personal lives at all. Some people are more affable than others and some will be more intimidated by your position than others. You must not push any of them. Let them open up to you in their own way until you know them well enough to know what they are thinking. If you become too familiar and speak to them as if you are their friend *before* they trust you, they may be insulted or they may simply choose to reject your advances. It's kind of like a first date Walter, if you come on too strong you might scare them off."

"Message received loud and clear, Josh," Walter responded with a smile.

"Its not all bad, Walter," Josh said. "Keep in mind that if you develop a close personal bond with any of your employees it will be that much more difficult for you to act as their boss in times of trouble. It is difficult to discipline a friend and even more difficult to terminate them. It's a fine line and one which all of us managers have difficulty walking from time to time."

Wanting to change the subject, Walter decided to ask Josh about those *toxic personalities* that they discussed during their first meeting. Walter recounted a story that had been bothering him. After his attempt at friendship in the lunchroom Karla had mentioned that Dick Yandeau, the fellow who got up and walked out on him, had been making some scurrilous comments about Walter to various people in the office. Rumor had it that Dick told a number of people that Walter was going to be fired and that it was just a matter of a few weeks before he was gone. He had also been spreading a rumor that the company was in trouble and that they would probably be bankrupt before the end of the year. He had even gone so far as to say that Craig Ferguson had been embezzling and that the police were investigating him. Walter knew that none of these things were true. He wondered if these were the ramblings of a crazy person or if Dick was one of those toxic people that Josh had spoken of.

Chapter 9

If I Can't Be Happy, Neither Can You

"I'm afraid that Dick sounds like someone with an extremely *toxic personality*, Walter," Josh began. "He could be miserable in his personal life and might just be acting out at work where he is safe from problems at home. That could be a result of some childhood trauma, a bad marriage, an unmanageable debt load or any number of negative psychological stimuli. Alternatively, he might just be the wrong person in the wrong job."

With that Josh reached into his desk drawer and pulled out a shiny new stainless steel nut and placed it on his desk. Then, he pulled out what appeared to be 2 identical bolts. He looked at Walter and asked, "These bolts looks like they should easily screw into this nut don't they?"

"Uh Huh," grunted Walter.

"Well here then, try to screw them together," Josh said challengingly.

Walter took the first bolt and put the nut up against it and began turning. Although the beveled end of the bolt fit nicely into the aperture of the nut, no matter how hard he pushed and turned, it would not grab the threads and allow it to enter. It was quite perplexing to Walter because for all the world, they looked like a perfect fit. He then took the second bolt which appeared identical to the first and attempted to screw it into the bolt. Much to his surprise, it fit perfectly and he screwed it in right up to the hilt.

"Okay, what's the trick here Josh?" Walter asked, laying the nut and bolt back on the desk.

"No trick, Walter. The first bolt is nineteen thirty seconds of an inch in diameter. The nut is nine sixteenth of an inch. That thirty second of an inch is just enough to prevent them from fitting together. The two bolts look the same because your eyes simply cannot discern such a tiny difference in diameter. You don't see many nineteen thirty second inch bolts you know. We have one brand of brake components that came in with nineteen thirty second bolts and nuts a few years ago and I kept a set in my desk along with the standard nine sixteenth variety, just in case I needed to make a point some day," Josh finished speaking with a wink and a smile.

"So what's the point, Josh?" Walter asked while doing a poor job of trying not to appear disinterested in these hardware items.

"The point my boy, is that you will never screw those mismatched nuts and bolts together any more than you will pound a square peg into a round hole or force an employee to fit into a job that they are fundamentally not right for. I could force that nut into that bolt using a vice and an impact wrench, but all that would accomplish is destruction of the nut and the bolt. Just like forcing someone to do a job that doesn't fit them will destroy them *and* the company they work for," Josh stated in a loud, confident voice.

Walter sat back in his chair simply saying, "Go on."

"Well," Josh continued, "often we find that when individuals are placed into a job that they are either not capable of doing or simply do not enjoy, they set up a defense mechanism which manifests itself as bad behavior. These people often believe that they are doomed to failure and want to make the company and everyone around them look bad in order to take the spotlight off of their own bad work. Sometimes they just feel unappreciated or disrespected because they are not getting pats on the back for their mediocre work They will criticize management, criticize others and generally blame everyone and everything for any number of real or imaginary problems. These folks come across as just plain miserable to most of their co-workers, but often there are a few other unhappy people in the workplace that they can turn to for vilification and sympathy. They hate to see others happy in the office and will do everything they can to change happy people into sad or angry ones. They will gather as many like-minded people as they can around them to launch a silent strike against management. God help you if you have a number of these types in your office, Walter. They could ruin you if you don't sort them out."

Walter was somewhat alarmed by Josh's frankness

ALWAYS REMEMBER: IF IT AIN'T FUN, IT AIN'T WORTH DOING

and pondered his first few weeks at Shelton Saunderson for a full minute before he responded, "So how do I sort them out, Josh?"

Josh sat back, breathed in, looked at the ceiling, interlocked his fingers and then looked Walter in the eye for a moment before speaking. "This is tough Walter," he stated. "You have to get into the minds of these people. You have to *coach* them into telling you what is wrong with them. They need to ferret out their own problems themselves."

"Jeez Josh, I can't remember any employee ever volunteering what might be wrong with them. That kind of goes against human nature doesn't it?" asked Walter.

"Well not really Walter," Josh said with a smile. "I think you would agree that most folks know what they want, wouldn't you?" Walter nodded and grunted, wondering what was coming next.

Josh breathed in and began again, "You must understand the basics of human nature. Everyone has values. They all have a primary belief in power, knowledge, religion, social welfare, beauty, harmony, the almighty dollar or a myriad of other things. Find out what drives them. Find out what their basic values are, Walter. Then, understand that those basic values drive them toward what they want from you.

Religious folks want order, tradition, and dogmatic methodology in the workplace. They are devoted to their religion and they enjoy its predictability. They thrive when they enjoy the same kind of environment at work.

Those that crave knowledge must be continually challenged. Don't let them stagnate in one job for too long.

Those that want power need to be allowed the opportunity to lead others in supervisory or management positions.

Those folks who bend toward social welfare want fairness and compassion in the workplace...for themselves to some extent, but mostly for others.

The ones who like sculpture, painting, crafts, and various other art forms will generally prefer a good deal of harmony in the workplace. You must find a way to provide it.

Contrary to what you might think Walter, folks who worship money above all, *do* have a place in your business. Those are the people who will sell the most product, make the best deals, and create the greatest profits. Not only do they like money in their bank accounts, but they want to work for a firm makes a lot of money too. They are your future sales leaders. Get into their heads Walter. Find out what they want."

"Whoo, that's kind of a tall order for a guy from Spruce River," Walter laughed.

"You will learn in time," Josh said with a smile. "Once you have discovered their values and wants, you will begin to recognize their corresponding behaviors. Simply put, people whose values are being satisfied and are getting what they want will exhibit good behavior. Those who are not getting what they want and feel that their values are being trampled will exhibit bad behavior. Behavior is either affirmation that we are getting what we want or an attempt at forced acquisition of what we want, but are not getting. Your friend Dick is exhibiting bad behavior because he is not getting what he wants. His attitude is a deliberate, yet stifled attempt to let you know that he wants something other than what he is getting out of life. Does that make sense?"

"Well, yes it does Josh," Walter said. "The problem is that I have absolutely no idea what he might want or how I might give it to him. I don't know what his values are and frankly he is such a grump, that I don't know if I ever will."

"Understood!" Josh stated emphatically. "Now the fun begins. You have to ask him questions. Ask him to describe the perfect job to you. Ask him what he likes best about his job. Ask him what he wants to do with the rest of his life. Then, ask him what is wrong with his job and what you can do to make it better. Use open ended questions so that he can't give you one word answers. Make sure he is forced to give you descriptive commentary. Above all, show a great deal of interest and let him do the talking. Whenever he gives you a clue as to what he wants, explore it and ask him what he is doing about getting there. If he can answer that, ask him how his attempts to get what he wants have worked for him so far. That way, he will be forced to examine his own actions and think about his own involvement in, and responsibility for his life struggles. Chances are he will admit that he has failed to work out a feasible plan that will enable him to succeed, and at that point you can sit down with him and help develop a blueprint for the future."

Walter spoke again, "What if he won't answer any of my questions?"

"Ah Ha! Now you are beginning to ask the right questions!" Josh laughed.

The older man sat back in his chair and looked at

Walter for a few seconds before saying calmly, "Then you let him go."

Surprised, all Walter could say was, "What?"

Sensing Walter's discomfort, Josh leaned forward and said, "Look here young fella, we can't save them all. Some folks are beyond our help. A percentage of people in the workforce simply hate their jobs and you have neither the time nor the qualifications to rehabilitate them. Many people are not suited to one job or the next and if they are not willing to talk to you about their inability to fit in at your shop, they are throwing down a challenge that you have no choice but to respond to. You must let them go so that you can get on with the business of building your business. And by the way, your other staff members will thank you."

"But people seem to like him. At least they spend time talking to him," Walter protested.

"That's typical," said Josh in a frank tone. "That kind of person always plays to an audience. They will be nice to the people around them so that they can enlist their army of **negativity soldiers** and launch an attack against you. The conversations they have generally involve a good dose of *boss-bashing* along with a considerable amount of criticism of the very company they work for. They actually seem to want to destroy the place where they make their living and they thrive on any amount of discomfort or stress that they can ladle over their employers.

You will hear them say things like, 'This Company doesn't care about us; things will never change around here; they can't get away with that; who do they think they are?' ...and so on and so forth. I don't suppose any psychologist or doctor has ever tried to come up with a cure for this disease Walter, but it sure is rampant in the workplace these days."

"So you think I should fire everyone that doesn't like their work, Josh?" Walter asked in a tone suggesting he didn't want an affirmative answer.

"No, no, no, you don't have to fire everyone. Very few people will refuse to respond to you if you give them a chance," Josh said, exasperated. "What I am saying is that you need to talk to them. Find out what is bothering them. Find out what they want out of life and out of their job and then try to help them. Often you will find that you can shift someone to a job within your own office that suits their values and wants and make a better employee out of them. You will also find that if you can adjust their job to suit their wants, you will soon have a happy, supportive employee who is more interested in building up your company than they are in tearing it down. When that happens, they will begin to wonder why they ever found fault with your Company in the first place and will do everything they can to make sure that it succeeds. Most importantly Walter, you will have created a new sense of loyalty towards you. They will begin to support you and build you up to the other staff. Then and only then will you begin building your own army. Your army will be built on positive emotion that will win out over attacks from all future negativity soldiers. So my young friend, what I am saying is that you must stop trying to pound square pegs into round holes. Find out what your people want and put them in their proper place. When you've done that, you will be amazed at how much better your business will run."

Josh sat back and pondered Walter's expressionless face for a moment. Finally he said, "Keep in mind too, that people generally do well when they get to do what they do best every day. That's your bonus. Your newly satisfied employee's will turn out more work and much better work with less effort, simply because they are enjoying it. Conversely, when you don't have the right people in the right jobs, the very best you can expect is mediocre results."

When Josh stopped speaking, Walter sat back in his chair thinking about what he had just heard. Josh felt it was time to break for the day, so he got up and politely held his office door open. Walter knew that was his cue to leave. Walter headed out the office door toward the showroom. He turned as he was passing Josh and lightly placing his hand on the older man's shoulder said, "This is good Josh. You have given me a lot to think about."

Josh smiled as Walter walked out through the big glass doors of the showroom. Knowing that Walter was on the verge of a major breakthrough, Josh was very pleased with the advice he had given him today.

Walter spoke very little at home that night. Sensing an uncharacteristic calmness in her husband, Lydia left him alone with his thoughts until it was time for bed. They ate a hearty meal of steak and baked beans for dinner that night. Lydia always believed that baked beans were comfort food and she could tell instinctively that Walter needed some comfort that evening. In bed later, as he lay on his back mesmerized by the blades of the revolving ceiling fan above, she kissed him on the forehead saying, "I think you are going to be okay, Honey."

"Thanks Baby. So do I," crooned Walter softly.

ALWAYS REMEMBER: IF IT AIN'T FUN, IT AIN'T WORTH DOING

With that Lydia turned off the lights, plunging them into the pleasing blackness of night. Curled up together in a loving embrace, they both slept soundly until the alarm sounded at 5:00AM.

Chapter 10

We Need to Talk

The next morning, Walter walked into his office building with an air of confidence in his stride while whistling the tune to the old ballad *"The Wild Irish Rover."* That song was something he recalled his father whistling or singing almost every day of his life. His dad, Dale always exuded a natural care-free confidence so it was almost like a right of passage that Walter would be whistling his favorite song this morning.

As he walked by Karla's desk Walter stopped whistling just long enough to say, "Good morning to you my dear friend." With that, he began whistling again and strode into his office. He plunked himself in his huge, high back leather chair and spun around in it twice before he noticed that Karla had followed him into the room.

"What in the name of God has gotten into you?" Karla asked in an incredulous tone.

"Nothing much," answered Walter with a smug smile. Before Karla had a chance to speak again he continued, "I just happen to believe I may have fallen face first into the secret to solving a lot of the problems around here. That's all!" he exclaimed.

"Well, I hope so, because if you haven't, you are making a perfect fool of yourself first thing in the morning," Karla said with a laugh. While squinting and curling up her nose she had to ask, "So what's the secret?"

"I can't tell you just yet. Please be patient until I know if it works and then I shall bare my soul to you," Walter stated calmly. "In the mean time, can you call Dick Yandeau and tell him that I would like to see him in my office in half an hour?"

"Sure thing!" exclaimed Karla as she spun on her heel and walked quickly back to her desk. She smiled to herself as she picked up her phone to call Dick. She had no idea what Walter was up to, but she felt in her heart that real change was beginning to happen.

When Dick arrived outside of Walter's office, Karla greeted him with a pleasant smile and said, "Go right in Dick. Walter is waiting for you." Dick was fearful yet defiant. He wasn't about to take any guff from this new upstart manager and yet he was harboring a feeling of dread. He feared that something bad was about to happen.

When the door opened, Walter immediately turned away from his computer so that he could give full attention to his visitor. "Come on in Dick, its great to see you again," he said genuinely.

Dick didn't know what to make of Walter's pleasant demeanor. He knew in his heart that his first meeting with him had not gone well and as he pondered what might be happening. His feeling of dread grew and he began to feel perspiration building on his brow. He curled his lips upward slightly in a failed attempt to smile. All he could manage to say was "Hello, Mr. Kennedy." Then he fell silent.

Sensing Dick's discomfort, Walter launched into the speech that he had been mentally rehearsing all morning. "So Dick," he began, "I imagine you are wondering why I called you here today." Dick nodded without speaking. Walter continued, "I know that you have worked here for fifteen years, but other than that, I don't know much about you. Because you are a long term member of the team here, I think it would help me to get to know you better."

At that, Walter paused and looked squarely into Dick's eyes. He could actually see the lines disappearing from Dick's forehead as his scowl disappeared. Walter was encouraged to see the beginnings of a half smile occurring on the other man's lips. It was evident that Dick was beginning to relax and was dropping his guard. Walter continued speaking, "Dick, I want to know everything about you…What you do, what you want to do, how you feel about the Company and how you think we can improve. Lay it all on me."

Dick began scowling again, his lips dropped back into a frown and Walter thought he had lost him. He knew instinctively that in his haste to put Josh's advice to work he had overwhelmed Dick with his overly intrusive enthusiasm. Finally after a frighteningly long pause,

ALWAYS REMEMBER: IF IT AIN'T FUN, IT AIN'T WORTH DOING

Dick began to speak, "So, did you call me here to decide whether or not you want to fire me?" he asked with virtually no expression on his face or emotion in his voice.

Walter thought to himself that this was going to be much harder than he originally imagined. "What have I gotten into here?" he thought to himself. He knew he had to reel Dick back in and to do that he had to start over by laying all of his cards on the table.

"Okay, Dick. I can see that we have started on the wrong foot, so let's try this again," he started. "Honestly, I have a feeling from what I have heard and observed that you really don't like me much and that you don't really like much about this Company either. Is that a fair comment?"

Dick leaned forward, peered directly into Walter's eyes and said, "Well Mr. Kennedy, I don't know who you have been talking to, but I love this Company and I don't know you well enough to dislike you yet, so I think you are badly informed."

Walter knew Dick was holding back but decided to soften his approach. "Okay Dick, let's move on. Tell me what you do here at Shelton Saunderson," he said in a soft, kindly voice.

"I am a senior policy analyst in our marketing department. I write wordings for new products and I review and update all of our in-house programs and policy forms as required. Sales people and marketers call on me constantly to explain forms and wordings to them and I often have to sit in at client meetings to bale out the sales guys who don't understand our products. Basically I am a writer who deals in technical data and boring minutiae," he said in a low voice.

"Great!" Walter said triumphantly before carrying on. "We need good technical people like you in our organization to keep our sales people on track. That must be satisfying work eh Dick?" He was so excited to have received a well thought out response from Dick that Walter seemed oblivious to his lack of enthusiasm for his job.

Dick sat back in his chair. Walter could see him squirming and looking around the room almost as though he was looking for an escape root. After a pregnant pause Dick said, "Not really."

"Oh," said Walter, thinking of Josh's advice. "So tell me why it's not satisfying, Dick. Based on your response it sounds like you don't like your work very much, so how can we make it better?" he asked.

Walter could see Dick's eyes widen and knew then that he had landed the hook squarely in his mouth. When Dick started speaking this time, the timber of his voice changed, the scowl left his face and he spoke in earnest, "The fact of the matter is that as much as I understand wordings and forms and I guess I am good at it, I find the whole job very boring. I am tired of explaining details to salesmen and I am tired of generating endless reams of paperwork that only serves to make other people look good. I feel like I am in the dark when it comes to what is important around here. I have become a mushroom in the bowels of this office and I need a change."

Surprised by Dick's candor, Walter shifted positions in his chair uncomfortably while stalling for time. He realized that Dick was probably in the wrong job but because of his attitude and behavior, Walter was still hesitant to consider changing his position. He thought of

Josh momentarily. That thought prompted him to ask the question, "What kind of change do you have in mind, Dick?"

Dick's interest in Walter's questions grew. He sensed that Walter was leading him to where he wanted to go in the conversation. "Well sir, I joined Shelton Saunderson years ago because I wanted to get into sales. I had a friend in sales here who has since moved on to another firm. He encouraged me to join as a trainee when I got out of college."

"So, why didn't you go into sales?" Walter interjected.

Dick began again, "Well, I applied for a sales trainee job, but when Craig Ferguson interviewed me, he told me that with my diploma in journalism, I belonged in the marketing department. Frankly I had no idea what the marketing department did and I was just happy to have a job. I have been there ever since."

"Did you ever ask to be transferred out of there before now?" Walter asked.

"Oh yes. I asked both Craig Ferguson and Jonesy to move me out of there on four separate occasions and all I ever got was, *'maybe someday.'* Then they would pat me on the back and tell me that I was doing a great job in marketing. Frankly I have given up," Dick said with a sigh.

Walter decided to take a chance by asking, "Why do you stay here Dick? Why don't you quit?"

Without thinking Dick immediately responded, "This has become my home, Mr. Kennedy. I like the people here. My best friends are here. Besides, this is the only place I have worked since leaving college, I can't imagine working anywhere else."

Walter was overcome with the realization that Josh was completely correct about putting people into the right jobs. Dick had been laboring away for years at a job he didn't like and the obvious result was bad behavior. All he wanted was someone to acknowledge that he wanted to do something else and give him a chance. The positive thing that occurred today was that Dick was willing to answer his questions and was very receptive to discussing the problem. He knew then that he would not have to let him go, and would instead probe further into the issues and help Dick come up with a plan for his career.

Walter asked some pointed questions about Dick's wants and values. In the course of that questioning, he uncovered some interesting things. Dick was very forthcoming and made it clear that not only did he want more money, but he wanted to feel the satisfaction of selling.

Walter knew that Dick had a great thirst for knowledge, which is what kept him in the insurance business, and made him extremely valuable to the firm. Most importantly, Dick cared about the people he worked with and he wanted to provide greater value to Shelton Saunderson. Walter could sense instinctively that Dick had a significant need for approval and acknowledgement that was not being satisfied in his current position. As the two men spoke to each other, Dick warmed up to Walter. At the same time Walter realized that there was much more to this once-scowling man than he had ever imagined. Over the next hour as Dick relaxed into the conversation, it became clear that he had a deep understanding of the insurance business and the psychology of sales. As the time passed, Walter also found that Dick had a great sense of humour and quite an affable charm. Before Dick was finished expressing himself, Walter had already decided to move him out of his current job and into sales.

It was clear that Josh had been right once again. When Walter peeled away Dick's outer armor, he uncovered a man who was not at all happy in his job. However, he clearly had the desire, the knowledge and the natural ability to become a better employee in another job.

Walter felt an almost sickening twinge of delayed emotion when he realized that he entered the meeting that morning quite prepared to let Dick go. Had he not followed Josh's advice and asked some important questions, he might have lost this loyal, long term employee.

Because of his intimate knowledge of all of the Shelton Saunderson programs and his ever growing devotion to the firm, Dick would go on to become one of the most respected sales rep's in the business. Walter was initially worried that his first convert might not be able to make it in sales, but Dick proved that his fears were groundless. In a short few months he would be hitting all of his sales goals and would eventually have the largest portfolio in the Company. In years to come, he would become one of Shelton Saunderson's most trusted employees and a member of the senior management team.

This was Walter's greatest personal victory to date at Shelton Saunderson. He knew that he owed it all to Joshua O'hare so as soon as Dick left his office; he called Josh to tell him the good news.

Chapter 11

The Essential Trait of Successful Managers

When Walter called Josh this time, he wanted to do something special for him so he decided to ask him out for a nice dinner. Josh was thrilled at the Walter's generous offer and accepted immediately. Much to Walter's surprise when he asked Josh what he wanted to eat that night, Josh picked sushi. Walter also enjoyed sushi but he never took Josh for a man who might like to eat raw fish. As he pondered Josh's choice, he realized that he had made an assumption based on nothing but his personal perceptions of Josh without any concrete evidence or information. This was exactly what he done with Dick. At that moment he realized that not unlike most of the people he had ever known, he wrongly believed that he could size people up and categorize them in a very short time with little or no information. He vowed to himself at that moment not to make unfounded assumptions about another person ever again.

The two men had agreed to meet at the Suzoran Sushi House on Pembina Street at 7:00PM. As Walter walked toward the door of the restaurant he spotted Josh pulling into the adjoining parking lot in a bright red, 1963 split window Corvette. Walter knew right away that this was a pristine, classic collector car and he smiled with some degree of pride to know that his friend, Josh would own such a beautiful driving machine.

"Wow, nice wheels Josh!" Walter called out as Josh walked toward him.

"Nothing like it!" Josh yelled back. When Josh drew near Walter both men's right hands instinctively lifted from their sides and met in a hearty handshake.

"So you like my Vette do you, Walt?" Josh asked with pride.

"Oh Yah!" Walter said enthusiastically.

"I only drive that car on special occasions or when I just feel like driving for the sheer joy of it. For my money, the Corvette is not only a classic American sports car. Pound for pound it might just be the world's best example of pure driving pleasure. I just love it. In fact I own four of them, all in different model years. I bought every one of them from the auto wreckers and rebuilt them from the frame up. It's a hobby of mine," Josh said with a big smile.

"I hope some day I can own one as nice as that," Walter said with clear envy in his voice.

"If you play your cards right, Water maybe some day you can have one of mine," Josh said with a laugh.

Walter grabbed Josh's upper arm saying, "Oh Please!" Josh laughed again as the two men entered the restaurant.

They were escorted to their table by a pretty Asian girl in a beautiful silk kimono. Walter was impressed with the quality of the décor in this place and was even more impressed when a waiter came running from behind the bar, and through the busy restaurant yelling, "Mr. Joshua, Mr. Joshua, it is so nice to see you again!" Josh stood up so that he and Kiroshi the waiter could embrace. "We will make a special meal for you and your friend tonight, Mr. Joshua. Don't you worry, you will be impressed," Kiroshi said happily has he made his way back to the kitchen.

Josh explained that Kiroshi was not just the head waiter. He was actually the owner of the restaurant. Some years ago, Josh had met him at a high school play that their daughters were acting in and they struck up a conversation. They soon became friends and visited each other's homes for family dinners on a regular basis. That was how Josh acquired his love for sushi. Dinner at Kiroshi's home was always traditional Japanese and always extremely delicious.

Kiroshi was working in another restaurant in those days, but always wanted to open his own place. Unfortunately because he was new to the country, he had no credit rating and was unable to find financing. Josh liked Kiroshi and trusted him, so he loaned him the down payment and then took him over to his bank, where he co-signed for a mortgage on the restaurant. He knew it was a risk, but he saw something in Kiroshi that appealed to him and he wanted to help. Within two years Kiroshi

ALWAYS REMEMBER: IF IT AIN'T FUN, IT AIN'T WORTH DOING

paid Josh back his entire down payment with interest and his restaurant became one of the top dining spots in the city. As he listened to this story, Walter's opinion of Josh moved even higher than it already was.

He couldn't wait to tell Josh about his meeting with Dick, so as Kiroshi brought course after course of sashimi, sushi, tempura and other exotic delights, Walter described every moment of his morning meeting.

Josh listened intently to Walter and was truly very proud of his young friend. He could see that Walter had a natural understanding of human nature and a great love of people. This he thought, was the person who could take over his business when he retired. He could easily take Joshua's Tire Centre to the next level of success. Walter could take the firm to national prominence and even become a force in major markets around the world. That thought was quickly pushed away when Walter said, "I just wanted to say thank you for being so helpful to me, Josh." Joshua was humbled by Walter's gratitude and he graciously accepted it before moving on.

Josh lowered his head in thought momentarily before saying, "You know what Walter? You have started something with Dick that you will have to finish."

Walter knew he was in store for another lesson from Josh, so he sat back and listened while sipping his green tea. It occurred to him that he had a lot to learn at this point in his career and Josh had not steered him in the wrong direction yet. He felt a bond with this man that transcended their ages and occupations. To Walter, Josh was a fount of business knowledge and someone he couldn't help but admire and respect.

Josh continued on, "Let me ask you a question, Walter. What is the number one essential trait of managers? And before you answer, let me clarify by saying that I am talking about *successful* managers."

Walter thought for only a second before saying, "The number one trait of successful managers must be the ability to manage."

"That's great Walt," Josh said sarcastically before carrying on. "You have just answered that you have no idea what I am talking about. Now I will ask you again, what is the essential trait of successful managers?"

This time Walter gave it a little more effort. He looked around the restaurant while thinking. He spotted Kiroshi explaining something to one of his waiters while carrying several plates to the kitchen. He blurted out "I've got it this time! The number one essential trait is knowledge. Managers have to know how to do everything so that they can set a good example and train their staff properly."

"Nope, try again." Josh said quietly.

Frustrated, Walter said, "Okay let me see. It must be experience, or maybe intelligence. Perhaps it is the ability to understand what other people want! I don't know, Josh. Give me a hint!"

Josh laughed and said, "How about I just give you the answer?" Walter smiled from ear to ear when he heard that. He was frustrated and a little embarrassed, but he was determined to get the answer to this most important of questions.

Finally Josh said, "The number one essential trait of successful managers is, **the desire to see others do well.**"

The answer didn't immediately strike Walter as being the correct one and he protested by asking, "Josh, what good is the desire to see others do well if I am not good at my job or I don't know what my employees want?"

Josh spoke again, "Look Walter. It is a given that managers generally have experience, knowledge and intelligence. What they don't always have is the desire to see others do well. They often only want to see *themselves* do well. They use their employees as vehicles to further their careers with no regard for the success of those employees. What many managers are missing is that if employees are not doing well in their jobs they will only turn out mediocre results. With mediocre results, no one in the firm will ever be really successful. Managers need to be selfless. If they spend all of their time assisting others to do well, with little regard for their own personal success, they will become successful despite their lack of ego. This theory has been proven over and over again. Virtually every successful self made business person, athlete or military leader I have ever met has been simple, humble and helpful. In other words, Walt those great men and women were selfless. They reveled in the success of others and they seldom thought about themselves."

Josh sat back for a moment, contemplating the broken tea leaf fragments at the bottom of his cup while regrouping his thoughts. After a short pause he said, "Walter, please accept that once your employees understand that your one undeniable driving force is the desire to see them do well, they will follow you to the ends of the earth. There will be no negativity and there will be no need to fear failure. Their attitudes will be turned from disengagement and procrastination to hard work and cooperation. Your selfless leadership will be the fuel that fires the engine of success. Your entire team will feel the power of teamwork and they will no longer tolerate mediocrity. They will be determined to win at all costs in order to gain your favor. *That*, my friend is what leaders do and *that*; Walter is how you must lead if you really want to turn your office around."

"Wow, that's pretty powerful stuff, Josh," Walter said in an almost incredulous tone. "How does one recognize a selfless leader?" he asked naively.

"Lots of ways," said Josh before continuing on. "Firstly, please understand that selfless people generally accept the belief that the legacy they leave behind will simply be the sum total of the good deeds they did during their lives. They will own some nice things, but they won't try to overdo their lifestyle. They won't live in a mansion on a hill and they won't ride around in chauffeur driven limousines. You will not find them wearing silk suits in an environment that calls for overalls. They are humbled by their success and they don't like to display their wealth for others to see. You won't find them coming in late and leaving early. They will be there everyday all day and will work harder than anyone in the place. They will know how to do virtually every job or be willing to learn, and they won't be afraid to roll up their sleeves to help out with the most menial of tasks. They will have employee assistance programs in place and they will have fair compensation at all levels. They will be approachable and virtually every one of their employees will feel comfortable calling them by their first name. They will understand that they do not have a monopoly on good ideas and will listen to recommendations from anyone who wishes to offer a thought. They will lead by example and will be an

ALWAYS REMEMBER: IF IT AIN'T FUN, IT AIN'T WORTH DOING

integral part of the working team. They will be respected and spoken of highly by their entire staff. They will consider all employees at all levels as equals. They will recognize good performance and will routinely compliment individuals and teams for good work. Above all Walter, they will treat every one of their people with a high level of respect. In short, the best managers *love* the people that work for them and will spend all of their time helping them to improve."

"Kind of like you eh, Josh?" Walter asked.

"Oh I don't know about that," Josh responded quickly.

"Well let's think about that for a minute," Walter said with a sly grin before continuing. "You have the happiest employees in town and they all call you by your first name. You have a one armed mechanic, Chad who couldn't find a job anywhere else but has done fabulously well with you. You have pictures of your employees plastered all over your office, but I couldn't find a single picture of you anywhere in the place. You told me about what a great guy Kenny the mechanic who fixed my ball joints was...just loud enough for him to hear. You drive an old Corvette that you bought from the wreckers and rebuilt yourself rather than simply paying a small fortune for one that was already done up, which is something you could easily afford. And now, Josh you tell me that you put this Kiroshi fellow into business at great financial risk to yourself, just because you liked him. No where in your story did I hear that you profited for Kiroshi's success and clearly the guy loves you to death. It seems to me that you are registering a ten on the selfless leader scale."

With that Walter stopped speaking and shot Joshua O'Hare a challenging smile. Without missing a beat, Josh immediately responded, "You do what you have to do, Walter. I don't go looking for credit for how I deal with people but I do like to think that I know what people want. If what I am doing works for them, then I am happy. No need for any pats on the back though, Walt. It's just life and we all have to live it our own way."

Walter could see the flush of embarrassment on Josh's face and out of respect for the older man he decided to change the subject. During the years to come, he would learn that the best leaders are a little uncomfortable with their own success and often find themselves embarrassed when it is pointed out to them. True leaders are really only excited by the success of their team and are often not even aware of the greatness of their own personal accomplishments. For them, the only successful events are team events.

"I understand the concept of selflessness Josh and I will try to live up to it, so help me with this one if you can. I have made the decision to move Dick into sales. I don't see him as a strong natural sales type, but I do see him as a credible purveyor of insurance products, if you know what I mean. In other words he is not a great talker and he is not naturally dynamic, but when he speaks he is so knowledgeable, believable and trustworthy that I think anyone would want to buy from him. How do you think I should handle his transition into the new job? In fact, most of my sales people seem a little aloof. How do you think I should handle them?" Walter asked sincerely.

"You better order another pot of tea, Walt," Josh said with a smile.

Chapter 12

Minders and Finders

After taking a few sips of the fresh tea, Josh thought for a moment and then said, "I have a lot of salesmen in my company so I have some idea of what you might expect from Dick. I have my counter sales clerks, which would be similar to your home and automobile insurance sales people. In addition to them I have 20 wholesale sales people who sell on the road to various dealerships in a four hundred mile radius. Those would be equivalent to your outside commercial sales people. I even have one guy who sells to other countries. He sells tires all over the Pacific Rim. That's a comparatively new venture but it is working out very well for us. I am hoping to expand on that in the future by moving into the European Common Market."

Josh was looking for a glimmer of interest from his young friend as he spoke about his company. Secretly, he wanted Walter to come to work for him, but he wanted it to be Walter's idea.

Oblivious to Josh's secret thoughts, Walter still yearned for greater knowledge of how to handle Dick and all of his other salesmen. "With that kind of sales force, you must have some great ideas about what makes sales people tick, Josh. Please tell me how you handle them all," He asked respectfully.

Pushing a piece of rice around with a chopstick, Josh spoke while staring down at his plate, "I don't handle them at all, Walt. They handle themselves." He looked up at Walter with a mischievous smirk on his face.

"Come on, Josh help me out here. This is one of the biggest problems I have at the office. We are a sales driven business and frankly I don't understand the sales people that work for me. They seem either flippant or completely aloof. I just don't know what drives them!" Walter complained.

"All right, all right, let me try to shed some light on the subject. But keep in mind that I am really not a salesman myself. I sell things, but I am not a salesman. Does that make sense?" Josh asked, wanting Walter to dig deeper.

"Kind of," Walter responded before asking, "In your mind, what *is* a salesman?"

"I have been asking that question myself for many years," Josh said sincerely before moving on with his explanation. "I have come to the conclusion that there are three types of sales people. The first type is easy to figure out. Some folks simply don't have the ambition or basic ability to sell anything to anybody. They are *non-sales* people and should not be involved in sales. The other two types are **minders and finders.**"

"Okay, Josh. I'll bite. What the heck are *minders and finders?*" Walter asked with a giggle in his voice.

Josh went on to explain that *minders* are people just like himself. They are relationship builders who form solid personal bonds with their customers. *Minders* are seldom outgoing or aggressive people and they don't like to be the centre of attention. They are instead more conservative and generally like the customer to do the majority of the talking, while they listen. Good *minders* will speak when asked for advice and will know their products intimately. They will not make assumptions and they will always ask for direction rather than taking the lead. In short, they will practice servant leadership, working on behalf of the client but never controlling the relationship.

Despite their apparent reticence and hesitance to take charge, they will fight to get the best deal for their customer and they will fight to keep from losing them to a competitor. Their clients will love them and trust them to do the right thing for them at all times. They are masters at building customer loyalty and they will generate sales revenue from the same group of customers year in and year out. Because of their steadiness, they will seldom lose a customer.

The main challenge for *minders* is that they have trouble attracting new customers in a competitive sales environment because they are uncomfortable with prospecting and cold calling. They have trouble asking for an order from a stranger because they have a great fear of rejection. Relying on *minders* to grow a business on their own would be a mistake. Conversely, relying on *finders* to keep a business strong would be equally foolish. A business requires a healthy mix of *minders and finders* in order to be successful.

Walter listened intently until Josh paused to take a sip of tea. At that point he asked, "So can you give me some examples of *minders and finders?*"

"Well Walt, I am a *minder*, and I would say that you are a *finder*. Let me tell you about both types and you can tell me if you agree," Josh said before quickly continuing. "I say that I am a *minder* because I really don't like making cold calls or initiating sales conversations. I realized that this would be a problem for me when I was in my twenties. After college, I got a job as an advertising salesman for the newspaper in my hometown. My job was to get business people to buy adverting in the paper by whatever means I could. I had no training and no mentoring from anyone. I knew that simply walking into a business and asking the manger to buy advertising from me would be far too daunting. I have never been good with confrontation or rejection and I was afraid. I was painfully shy in those days, so I decided that it would be easier to make telephone sales calls. That way I could sell advertising without ever actually having to look my prospects in the eye. I still didn't do very well, because I would procrastinate all day, finding completely ineffective things to do rather than making phone calls. I would read junk mail, send memos, chat with the other staff, make personal calls or just stare out the window. I would do almost anything to avoid picking up the phone. After a few months, the sales manager let me know that I wasn't working out. After a good conversation with him, I agreed that finding and selling new accounts was not my strength and I agreed to resign.

ALWAYS REMEMBER: IF IT AIN'T FUN, IT AIN'T WORTH DOING

He suggested that I get into retail sales where clients would come to me to buy things without my having to make any difficult calls. I took his advice and here I am today."

Walter was thinking to himself that not only was he surprised that this great man was afraid of confrontation and rejection, but also that he could not relate to any of the issues that Josh had with sales. In Spruce River he always dropped into every new business that opened because he didn't want to miss the opportunity to meet the owner and try to sell him insurance. In his mind, the clients had always been happy to see him and the visits always went well. "How strange that we see things so differently," he thought.

Josh's admissions that he was fearful of selling made Walter admire him even more. It suddenly occurred to Walter that what made Josh great was his incredible sense of self-awareness. He always exhibited humility and concern for others, and he carried no ego or conceit. He was completely comfortable when admitting his own weaknesses and he was happy to share his personal fears. Walter thought that Josh must know himself so well that he was always able to avoid the pitfalls of trying to be someone that he is not. That strength also allowed him to avoid the hazard of trying to impress people with skills, talents, or qualities that he may not have. By admitting to himself what he is not particularly good at, Josh was able to eliminate ineffective activities and attitudes from his life. Because of the lack of pretense in his life he was able to focus only on positive things in areas where he has natural strengths.

Because of his admiration for Josh, later in his life,

Walter's personal motto would become, *"The difference between mediocrity and greatness is self awareness."* He would use that statement as his personal motto and he would live it to the fullest.

Joshua continued, "Although I was a sure-fire failure as a salesman, I thought that if I had something good to sell and a good location, I could make a living. At one point or another, I noticed that there were thousands of tires rolling past me on cars all day long. I thought about how many millions of tires there must be just in North America alone. I knew that there were summer tires, winter tires, all season tires, car tires, and truck tires. I also knew that they all had to be replaced every few years. I thought that even a lousy salesman like me should be able to sell such an incredibly universal product. After some research, and some help from a friendly banker I opened my first shop in the same location where you and I first met. I have never looked back, Walter."

"So, I would imagine that since you are a *minder*, you have plenty of repeat customers?" Walter asked.

"Oh yes," Josh said with pride. "I seldom lose one. If I have one thing to be proud of, it is the fact that my customers come back for new tires year after year. We work very hard at giving them the best service we can. My employees treat them well and I like to help out wherever possible. I like to meet as many customers as I can in the course of the day. That's how I met you, Walt."

Walter was happy with Josh's explanation of *minders*, but he wanted to hear more about *finders*. Since Josh had identified him as one of those, he *had* to know more. "So tell me about *finders*, Josh," Walter pleaded eagerly.

"Well, from what I have learned about you so far Walt, I see you as a strong *finder*," Josh started. "You have that outgoing, affable charm that most *finders* have. You are so optimistic and trusting that you can't even imagine that any prospective client might not want to deal with you. In your mind, you have something that they need and you are the best person for them to buy it from. You trust everyone to treat you with respect and because of your self confidence and charm, they generally do. You seldom, if ever suffer from call reluctance and you land the majority of accounts that you prospect. Unless I miss my bet, I would wager that you are thrilled with every new account you win and that you compete with everyone around you to be the top sales person in your field."

Feeling the need to interrupt, Walter said, "Wow Josh, I don't know how you came up with all of that after knowing me for only the short time that you have."

"Am I right?" Josh asked.

Walter looked the older man square in the eye saying, "Well I guess so. I have never thought of it in those terms, but I do like selling and I like to win, so I if that's what makes a *finder*, then I suppose I am one."

"By the way, Walter I suspect that your sales success played a huge part in your promotion to senior management at Shelton Saunderson," Josh commented confidently.

"So it's a good thing then?" Walter asked.

"Not always," Josh said emphatically. Seeing Walter's lips curl downward he continued, "The fact of the matter is that I find that really strong sales people are often only driven by personal gain. Remember what I said about successful managers earlier. They put the team first. We often see the opposite with strong sales folks. Some of the best sales people work alone, considering themselves first and foremost. Their team is secondary and often given no consideration at all. They can produce incredible amounts of revenue both for themselves and your firm. However, because they guard their relationships with their clients and avoid sharing information with their co-workers, they make it difficult for their managers to control their activities. I am sure you have often heard about sales people leaving their employers and taking hundreds of thousands of dollars worth of sales revenues with them. That is the greatest fear of many sales managers. The sales person's desire to protect their portfolios can be so overwhelming that they become distant and removed. In the long term, their actions may be detrimental to the development of a great working team or of a consistent and loyal client base.

"Gee, Josh. I hope you don't think that I am like that!" Walter complained.

"No I don't," Josh answered quickly. "I want you to understand that some of the best salesmen are loners, but some great salesmen are our future leaders. You have to learn to tell the difference. You, my friend are a team player and your number one driving force is the desire to make your team happy and successful. Clearly, that is why we are here tonite. That charming, affable confidence of yours wins people over. You make friends easily and you thrive on human relationships. I don't recall hearing even once since we met that you have any concern over your own pay check or your own level of success. That is what Craig Ferguson saw in you too. You have a once in a lifetime combination of qualities. You are a great salesman with a great sense of teamwork. That combination will make you a great leader of people, Walter."

This time it was Walter's turn to blush. He was more than a little shocked by this huge compliment from this great man. In order to create some time to think, he slurped a big mouthful of green tea before speaking. Once he composed himself he said, "Thanks for that, Josh. I really appreciate the compliment." After Josh nodded and smiled his acknowledgement of his young friend's appreciation, Walter continued, "Now, I am having trouble understanding why I would want any of those self centered, ego-centric sales types that you described working for me at all."

"Oh you need them all right," Josh said calmly. "The reason you need them is that without *finders*, your *minders* will have little to do. Yours is not a simple retail business where clients are attracted to a location or a product line. You are selling a complex service that requires a great deal of specialized training. That being the case, in order to differentiate themselves from the herd, your salespeople have to be the best and your service people must be even better. Let's take Dick Yandeau as an example. From the way you have described him, he will be a great *minder*. He has all of the technical knowledge he needs, he likes to help others, and he is devoted to the firm. However, he probably does not have the natural tenacity to chase down new clients and move them to your firm. Dick will eventually begin to attract new clients through referrals from existing customers, but it will be years before he brings in the large volume of new customers that will be necessary to grow your business. You need *finders* to provide a constant supply of new customers. Many *finders* however get bored with dealing with the same people year in and year out because they prefer the adrenalin rush they get from landing new accounts. Some have no use for *after-sale service* either. They don't consider anything that is non-remunerative to have any value at all. Always remember that successful people get to do what they do best every day. When people are forced to do tasks that they have no interest in or aptitude for, their ambition will wane and their results will diminish. Let your *finders* locate your new customers and let your *minders* handle the service. That is the natural order of things.

The best thing you could do is put Dick in as a back up account manager to one of your best *finders* for the first while. Have your *finder* introduce Dick and make it clear to the clients that if they can't get in touch with the *finder* for any reason, Dick is there to help out. In no time at all, those clients will be calling him exclusively. They will become devoted to their *minder* and claim him as their own. Dick will become equally devoted to his clients because he will feed off of their faith in him and he will fight to keep them in the fold. When that happens, the original *finder* will have lost his hold on them and you will have far fewer fears about losing revenue if he or she quits and goes to work for a competitor."

"That's great. In fact, it's almost a little diabolical," Walter said with a smile.

"I think it's just good common sense," Josh replied with conviction.

Josh called Kiroshi over and asked him for the bill. Almost as a silent testament to their mutual respect and generosity, when the bill reached the table both men reached for it at the same time. Walter politely explained that he had asked Josh to dinner and that it was his obligation to pay. Josh accepted his young friend's point of view and allowed him to place his credit card in the leather bill holder that Kiroshi left on their table. They walked out of the restaurant together and as they stood in front of Josh's Corvette, the two embraced in a show of unexpected emotion that could only come to people who truly cared about each other. A handshake would have been far too insignificant for two men who had opened up so much to each other. As Walter listened to the deep throated roar of the exhaust from Josh's Corvette as it sped away, he felt very good about himself. He knew that he was finally making progress and was looking forward to returning to work.

Chapter 13

Clear Expectations

One morning a month after his last meeting with Joshua O'Hare, Walter decided to spend some time walking around the office chatting with the staff to see if things had improved at all. He was pleased that several employees greeted him with a smile or a friendly, **Hello**. Walter was a little surprised at the new and improved attitude of many of his team. He did not know it at the time, but Dick Yandeau had already begun spreading the word about his meeting with Walter.

Dick had moved from an air of abject negativity to one of pure positive energy. The people who knew him best were pleased by the sudden improvement in his demeanor and were fascinated by his change in attitude toward Walter Kennedy. Dick spent no time at all announcing his promotion to the sales department and he lavished praise on Walter with everyone he talked to. The former Captain of the **negativity soldiers** had left that army and joined Walter's team. Unbeknownst to Walter, Dick was committed to making things better and would work tirelessly to make improvements happen in years to come.

Walter felt that he needed to get to know his senior people better so he called a meeting of the various department managers and supervisors later that morning. He had no idea what he was going to say to them but he had always had a gift for thinking on his feet and he knew that *something* would come to him when he needed it. He decided to invite Karla on the guise of taking minutes, but he really wanted her there for moral support. He also invited Dick Yandeau so that he could formally announce his promotion and see how that decision would go over with the management team.

As the managers and supervisors filed into the Shelton Saunderson boardroom he noticed that they did not seem as warm and friendly as the staff members that he had spoken with earlier. These people seemed just as cold and distant as they were the day he moved into his office. His heart sank a little, but buoyed by his last conversation with Josh, he immediately began thinking about what his next move should be.

Once everyone was seated, he acknowledged Karla and let everyone know that she would be taking the minutes of the meeting. Next he introduced Dick as the newest addition to the sales team. He explained that he wanted to expand the sales department and was sure that Dick would be a great fit. The group generally smiled politely but not a word was spoken by anyone.

"What is wrong with these people?" he thought to himself. This was one of the most awkward moments he had suffered through at Shelton Saunderson to date. He felt the need to end the silence, so he decided to speak about the direction he wanted the company to take.

"So...the reason I have asked you all here today is to talk to you about what I want Shelton Saunderson to look like in five years," he began.

As he spoke, he looked around the table for any sign of interest from the assembled throng of leaders. Seeing none, he continued on, "I want to take us out of the dark ages and into the light. We need to start making more sales, eliminate unnecessary expenses, and improve the bottom line. My goal is that at the end of five years, we will have increased our sales revenues by thirty five percent and increased our profit margin by fifteen percent." At that point he stopped and looked around the table. Reactions to his comments were mixed.

He saw some approving smiles, some blank stares and occasional frowns. He decided to carry on, "I really don't want to reduce staffing because I think all that would accomplish is to increase the workloads of the remaining staff and reduce their effectiveness. Besides, I have always believed that staff cuts are a defensive move. If we want to move forward in a positive fashion and boost the bottom line, we need to make offensive plays. That being the case, I think we can cut a small amount on the operating expense side, but we have to make it up on the sales side. We need strong sales people bringing in new customers and good service people like Dick maintaining our current client base. We need to impress every customer we meet with the sheer majesty of our service levels and we must always price our products competitively. In short folks, *we must be the best.*"

Walter's voice cracked on the last word so he stopped and waited for a glimmer of interest from the group. His solitary discussion finally ended when one of the managers spoke up.

Rick Rogers, the head of Shelton Saunderson's marine division had something on his mind and he felt the need to be heard. "At the risk of sounding a little skeptical, Walter I have to say that as much as I appreciate your desire to move us out of the dark ages, I can't imagine that anything will ever really change around here," Rick stated matter-of-factly.

"Oh really, Rick...Why don't you share with us why you feel that way?" Walter asked.

Feeling the warmth of a blush coming to this face, but still ready for a fight, Rick Rogers continued on, "Well, I have been here for fifteen years and it has been made clear to me year in and year out that my job is to manage, not to think. I have been told to improve results but every time I try to come up with a new program I get shot down. I have been in this business for over thirty years and believe it or not, I do have some idea about what I am doing. And yet, I get no credit for the things I do. I don't feel like I am in charge of my own department and someone above me is always making decisions for me. Sometimes I don't find out about those things until months later. Senior management seems to want to micro-manage all kinds of little things, but don't want to communicate with me at all on what my job really is. I have lots of responsibility, but no authority, except when something goes really wrong. When that happens, all of a sudden it's all my fault. Frankly, I have no idea what you guys expect from me."

Walter was taken aback by Rick's honesty. He was also amazed that in the short time he had been the manager of the office, he had already become one of *'you guys'* and had to bear the weight of a lot of old history on his back. He could feel the frustration in Rick's words and knew that he had to address the issue. "So, do the rest of you feel the same way that Rick does?" he asked the group while making a point of scanning the faces of everyone at the table.

Some people nodded, some smiled, while some made quietly audible comments such as, "uh huh" and "yup."

Walter knew at that moment, he had stumbled onto one of Shelton Saunderson's biggest problems. The management team had been frustrated for years with a lack of authority and had been taking it out on their employees. If managers didn't have clear direction, how could they possibly be expected to provide clear direction to the people that worked under them? The result of this consistent lack of clarity was the poor morale that Walter had witnessed when he first entered the office. It was also the source of his constant concern and distress. He was suddenly overwhelmed by a feeling of great disappointment in all of his managers. He felt that they were the cause of every problem he had encountered so far. He wondered if he got rid of all of them, would things get better. *Cut off the head and the snake dies*, Walter thought fleetingly before putting that inappropriate negativity out of his head. Although it seemed apparent to him that these few managers had been holding their employees in a state of suspended animation for years, it was really not their fault. The problem stemmed from much higher up the corporate ladder.

The Board of Directors and senior management at Shelton Saunderson had not evolved along with the company. Over the past fifty years, the company had grown from one office to one hundred and seventy five, but senior management had not really changed at all. Henry Shelton in his late eighties was still the chairman of the Board. Henry's fifty-two year old son Bob sat next to him at the board room table. Justin Saunderson had died several years prior, but his younger wife Henrietta was a major shareholder and still maintained managing director status. In that role, Craig Ferguson was her direct report and she utilized him as her eyes and ears to the company. These three essentially controlled the Board of Directors and had always made sure that all other Board members were people that they approved of. They had tremendous business acumen and always put the company above everything else in their lives. Unfortunately though, they had gotten out of touch with day to day operations and did not really grasp the sheer size of their company. As a result, they allowed most of their offices to run quite independently but still tried to manage the head office as if it was their only office. It almost seemed as though they had lost control of almost *everything*, but felt a need to have direct management control over *something*.

Since their boardroom was in the original head office, that was the office that fell victim to their need for control. With little else to do, they spent far too much time trying to micro-manage the day to day operations there. Craig Ferguson was routinely called into impromptu Board meetings to discuss the state of the head office results. While he was there, he would be asked about current sales programs or who might be doing something wrong. Craig's reaction to these inquisitions was to treat his managers in kind. He made certain that Bob Jones kept all of the managers and supervisors in check and reported back to him on everything they did. No one was allowed to do anything out of the ordinary unless Craig Ferguson approved it. Because Craig was uncomfortable appearing before the Board, many good ideas were never acted upon. That lack of action and the ongoing lack of clarity finally drove Bob Jones to his current state of ill health and ultimately lead to his resignation.

Walter knew that he needed to have his managers and supervisors on his side, so he began by making a promise to them that he only hoped he could fulfill. "Rick, I understand where you are coming from, and I thank you for your honesty. I want all of you to understand that I am not Bob Jones or Craig Ferguson. I have a job to do here and I am promising you that from now on, I will provide clear expectations to each and every one of you. I want your input into every decision we make around here and my door is always open to new ideas. You will run your departments with full authority and I will act as a resource to you. If I can't make that happen I will have failed and I will resign." With that he stopped and scanned the room again. This time he saw nodding and he heard positive comments. "Great," one person said. "Wow," said another.

Rick Rogers sat back in his chair and smiled. He

pursed his lips while nodding his head, which was a clue to everyone in the room that he was going to speak again. He did not disappoint them.

"Well, Walter one thing is for sure. You've got guts. You just promised to resign if you can't do your job. I want you to know that I for one will support you, but I will also hold you to your promise if things don't work out." When Rick stopped speaking, he stared into Walter's eyes before smiling widely.

Walter acknowledged Rick's challenge with a chuckle and carried on where he left off, "I want to have interviews with each of you to discuss how your departments are doing and what we can do to improve things. I want each of you to come to these meetings with ideas of your own and I want you to tell me about any ideas you have had in the past that have been rejected. We need to start fresh and rebuild each of your departments with your own concepts. These meetings will also allow us to discuss your authority levels and allow an opportunity for me to provide the clear expectations that I believe you are all in need of. "What do you all think?"

This time the managers and supervisors all began speaking at once. Some of the comments that Walter could discern were, "That's great; just what I wanted to hear; thank goodness!" Walter was happy. He had succeeded in re-energizing his senior people and he felt good about it.

"Okay then, this meeting is over. I want to start the interviews right away, so I will be around to see as many of you as I can today, and I will carry on for the rest of the week until everyone has been heard from," Walter said, while standing up and pushing his chair toward the table.

In the course of his meetings, Walter would find out that most of his managers had no idea how well their respective departments were doing financially. This was a common thread. Those that had received even minimal financial information were sworn to secrecy by Bob Jones.

It was imperative to the Board that as few people as possible knew what the specific financial results of the company were. Their perspective was that it was *their* business and that there was no reason to let employees in on where the money was going. That secrecy kept the managers, and subsequently the staff from having any sense of success in their own accomplishments. It also prevented them from having any reason to try harder. It was very much like going bowling and not keeping score. They were all throwing balls and making occasional strikes, but no one really ever knew if they were doing well or not. Walter promised to give them copies of the monthly financial reports broken down by department. Every manager he spoke with was pleased with Walter's openness, but some were still a little skeptical.

Next he tackled job descriptions and role awareness. It soon became apparent that none of the managers or supervisors really knew what their job descriptions were or what senior management expected of them. There had never been any written job descriptions at Shelton Saunderson, so the managers just did what they *thought* they were supposed to do. Because of this haphazard management style, often when something went wrong, the line managers were immediately chastised by senior management for having stepped outside of their authority. Of course since they had no idea what their authority was, they had no idea when they might be off base. That created a lot of problems and a good deal of dissension. It also set each manager up for failure. How could they possibly be expected to succeed when they had no idea what success for them looked like?

In order to get the managers on track Walter asked them all to write out their own job descriptions and bring them to him by week's end. In order to improve their role awareness, he planned to review the descriptions and then let them know what *his* expectations were. That way, everyone would be totally clear on what their roles were and the expectations of management would be on record. Walter also asked each manager to perform the same exercise for each of their employees so that every person in the office would have clear expectations and ultimately a better sense of self worth.

During his discussions, Walter found out that several people had been fired over the years without ever really knowing what they had done wrong. These people had no concrete idea of what their responsibilities were or how well their departments were doing financially prior to the axe falling. There were no benchmarks, so no one really knew how much production was required or what the minimum requirements for quality were.

Terminations usually came as a surprise to everyone. No warnings were given and most of the terminated individuals were never really given a fighting chance to succeed. They were not told that their performance was unacceptable until the day they were let go. Walter was shocked to find out that performance reviews were never done on anyone. There was no standard performance review format and no one could recall ever having even had an informal performance review.

It sounded to Walter as though many of the people that had been terminated might have been saved if they had their jobs explained to them or if they had been made aware of why they were failing. He was sickened by what he heard.

One of the saddest things Walter discovered was that there was no recognition for a job well done. Management was as negligent in handing out compliments as they were in allowing their employees to fail without warnings. Those who did well only knew of their success through informal compliments from customers or co-workers. Management provided no reason for loyalty or initiative other than a paycheck.

Now that Walter was beginning to understand what the major underlying problems at Shelton Saunderson were he was more comfortable in his ability to improve things. He felt that he was going in the right direction, but he also felt the need to talk to his friend, Joshua O'Hare. He decided to stop at Joshua's Tire Centre on his way home from work that night.

When Walter walked through the doors of Joshua's Tire Centre it almost seemed as though Josh knew he was coming. Walter's favorite *"Joshua's"* employee, Karen told him to go right into Josh's office as soon as she saw him coming though the front doors.

"Hey Walt, long time no see!" Josh said with a chuckle as Walter settled into the client chair in front of his desk. "What's up my friend?" he asked in a pleasant but concerned tone.

"Well, Josh I had a meeting with my managers today and I believe I have uncovered some of the real reasons for the problems at Shelton Saunderson." Walter said confidently.

"Tell me more," Josh said, leaning forward with his hands outstretched in an obvious display of receptiveness. Walter told Josh the entire saga of his meeting with the managers and explained what he had heard during the interviews afterward. He spoke of his decision to share financial information and how he wanted to develop job descriptions and performance reviews. He proudly restated his desire to provide clear expectations and admitted his offer to resign if he failed. At that point Josh interrupted him.

"You offered to resign?" Josh asked in amazement.

"Yah, I did. I might have been grandstanding at the time, Josh but it just felt right to me. As much as I really don't want to resign, if I can't get that office turned around soon, I really don't think I will feel much like staying on," Walter responded defiantly.

"Well, Walt you can always come to work for me in my little tire business." Josh said in a serious tone. Walter smiled at the comment, still unaware that Josh was dropping a serious hint. Then he sat back in his chair, exhaling loudly.

Josh carried on, "Seriously, Walter you put your head into the lion's mouth this time. If you actually provide financial information to front line managers, Craig Ferguson will probably blow a gasket. He told me years ago that old Justin Saunderson was so tight lipped that no one other than the Board and their accountant knew how much anyone's salary was, let alone how much profit the company was making."

"I know, I know. The Board members are so controlling that it is amazing anything gets done at all. Poor Craig is just a pawn in their hands. Their hoarding of information and their need to micro-manage so much of what goes on has created an oppressive environment for everyone. Frankly, I started out being annoyed with the managers, but now I just feel sorry for them. I have to do *something* to get them back on track," Walter said firmly.

"I agree with you, Walter," Josh said encouragingly. "You have great instincts, you know. I must tell you that I hold a manager's meeting every month to review individual branch results and overall company financials. I only withhold information that my lawyers won't let me hand out. There are some things that must remain confidential I admit, but everything else is available to my team. I also insist that the managers share this information with their staff. I have job descriptions for every position in my company and we review those annually to make sure that they are still appropriate. I encourage my managers and staff to ask me questions about the financials and I often have calls or emails from various employees letting me know that something about their job description needs to be changed. My managers do performance reviews on everyone annually as a minimum, and my employees see what the managers write about them in the reviews. I want a completely **transparent** environment and I want decisions to be made from the bottom up. You and I think alike, Walt."

Walter took a second to absorb Josh's comments. It occurred to him that he had finally done something that Josh approved of but which Josh had not given him advice on before he acted. He was proud of that. "So tell me something, Josh. Since your have had a transparent environment for so many years, what can I expect to see from Shelton Saunderson in the future?" he asked.

"You can expect *FUN* Walter!" Josh said, emphatically while leaning forward in his chair. "When your team knows that you care about them and you have nothing to hide, the walls will be torn down and the fun can start. Your employees will begin to trust you unconditionally and they will open up to you. They will work hard to make sure that your company is successful and they will do everything they can to prove their loyalty to you. You must always practice persistent consistency. In other words you must be diligent and never waiver in your effort to be fair to everyone. In addition, providing clear expectations must happen constantly, not just occasionally. The wonderful thing Walter is that when all of these things start working for you, there will be a rapid and continuous improvement in your bottom line. Happy people are productive people after all. If the Board of Shelton Saunderson wants more profit, then they need to let you finish what you have started. Do you think they will be onside?"

Suddenly Walter was stricken with the realization that the Board might not support him in any of his new initiatives. That prospect quickly filled his mind with anxiety. "I don't know, Josh. I just keep thinking about my Dad who always said, *'If it ain't fun, it ain't worth doing.'* He really seemed to be having fun at work all of the time and frankly I haven't had a single day of fun since I moved here," Walter lamented.

Sensing Walter's pain, Josh wanted to improve his

mood. "Look, Walter you bit off even more than your Dad could chew when you took this job. I am sure that if he was in your place, he would be having the same problems you are. My God, I wouldn't want to trade jobs with you either. You are making great strides though and I think you will soon see some light at the end of the tunnel."

"I suppose you're right Josh, but my people seem to put up huge walls that are impossible to climb over," Walter complained.

"The reason they put up walls, Walter is decades of history. They don't trust the management at Shelton Saunderson because they are accustomed to seeing nothing happen. They would love to talk about career development, workloads, skills training and personal issues, but they are making the assumption that nothing will ever change. They see no need to make the effort. You have to break that down, Walter. You have to earn their trust," Josh said in a kindly manner.

"I know I have to force them to change their attitudes," Walter responded.

"Wrong!" Josh snapped. "You don't have to force them to do anything. They have to do it themselves. Everyone and everything travels towards its own destiny under its own power. The one thing in life that you have almost complete control over is your own destiny. If you make positive changes in yourself, your personal power will lead you to a good result. Always think positively and always make decisions based on good intentions. Any decisions you make because of anger, retaliation, or hatred will have negative results. When you control your own thinking rather than

ALWAYS REMEMBER: IF IT AIN'T FUN, IT AIN'T WORTH DOING

attempting to control the thoughts and actions of others, your leadership will shine through and others will follow. Eventually, your good example will become the model for your team. Everyone around you will be compelled to make positive decisions. The bottom line is that you must take direct control of yourself and you must always accept responsibility for your actions. Once you have embraced that concept, you must practice it consistently, never wavering. That is the reality for all real leaders. Now get back to work and have some fun Dammit!" Josh joked.

Walter laughed politely, but he really couldn't find any humor in his current situation.

Chapter 14

If It Ain't Fun, It Ain't Worth Doing

When Walter walked through the doors of Shelton Saunderson the next morning, he realized he had been working there for 9 months to the day. That prompted him to mentally evaluate his progress so far. He thought about those first days when no one wanted to talk to him and how unhappy everyone looked. He smiled when he thought about his successful meeting with Dick Yandeau and he laughed quietly to himself when he thought about his disastrous foray into the staff lunchroom.

He knew he had made some headway, but he also knew he had a fair distance to travel before he could relax completely. He felt that he was beginning to get the trust of the staff but to succeed completely he needed to deliver persistent consistency with his own management practices. It was imperative that his managers were on side so that they could assist him in improving the environment in the office. Now that he had gotten to know them better, he was actually quite comfortable with most of the management team but he would continue to have meetings with them to make sure they did not stray from the cause.

Walter began to think about the phrase that had been haunting him so much lately. *"If it ain't fun, it ain't worth doing,"* he mused. "What does that mean?" It was perhaps a silly thing that people just say for the sheer fun of it, but to him it had a much deeper and significant meaning.

He decided that fun was the essence of good health and good humor. People who are healthy and happy generally get more fun out of life than those who are ill or depressed. He also knew that many studies had indicated that people who are happy in the workplace are much more productive than those who are miserable. Happy people work harder because they are able to focus on their work without distraction. Their work means so much more to them than people with problems.

Walter concluded that if his people were not having fun, they would never reach the level of profitability that the Board required. "If they don't have fun, they will never attain their goals and then *'it'* really won't be worth doing."

He smiled as he thought about how he had done such a thorough job of analyzing the silly old saying that he had heard his Dad repeat so many times as he was growing up in Spruce River. He also considered the fact that his new mentor, Joshua O'hare had used the same expression during their first meeting. It seemed clear to

Walter that a good deal of Josh's success in business could be attributed to the fact that he believed that he must create fun in the workplace everyday.

Walter knew that he had to have a clear understanding of what makes people happy. Fun was more than just activities and games that make people laugh. He realized that fun is borne of honesty, clarity, consideration, compassion, and respect for others. When those things are present, peace of mind is allowed to exist. In that mental state, happiness will naturally flourish and grow. Fun is that special ingredient that healthy, happy people carry with them at all times. People we look up to, people that others wants to get to know, people who have many friends. These people seem to have fun all day, everyday. Happy people enjoy telling others that they love their jobs. They are pleased to announce that they are glad to be able to go to work every morning. They love the people they work with and they love the work they do. *Life* is fun for them.

He considered that stress or more correctly, *distress* is one of the greatest and most universally accepted killers of fun in the workplace. He knew that he must make his workplace comfortable for all who were employed there. He must always assure that the expectations that he and his managers have for their workers are fair and reasonable. Shelton Saunderson must not be responsible for creating stressful situations for its workers. People who are working under stress for any reason are not capable of creating or enjoying any fun that may exist in the office. As a result, they will not be totally productive and they will be a burden to their coworkers. He knew that he would never be able to eliminate stress completely, but he could make it a priority to be conscious of the needs of his workers in order to avoid creation of stress wherever possible.

When Walter was a young lad in school, he observed the fact that fun was contagious. His good humor made other people smile and laugh. He had also noticed that bad humor and bad attitudes were just as contagious. He knew that he had to set the example at Shelton Saunderson. He had to present an image of good humor and happiness at all times. He must never allow his personal problems to impact on his relationships with his employees and he must never allow negativity to be the driver behind any management decisions that he might make.

Drawing on the things that he learned from Josh, Walter knew that he must make sure that he had the right people in the right jobs. He knew that in order to do that, he had to train his management team to ask probing questions to determine what skill sets and aspirations each employee might have. He must create teams of people who enjoy their jobs and who have a clear understanding of what is expected of them. His employees must understand the vision of the company and how they fit into it. Most importantly, the employees must know how well the company is doing and how they can contribute to its success. Walter understood that almost all people inherently want to do well. The best way to get the best from them was to trust and respect them enough to let them know when they were doing well and when they were not.

He thought back to his time in the logging industry. He remembered how the loggers all looked after each other and how they all knew instinctively what their jobs were. He remembered the friendship and fun that the men had with each other. Despite the inherent dangers in the woods, those men still managed to enjoy each others company and have fun everyday. He fondly remembered his friend, Buffalo teaching him about barber's chairs and schoolmarms. *"Buffalo"* he thought. "What a great man." His eyes became clouded with joyful tears as he thought about the lessons he had learned from his old friend.

His mind wandered back to present time and Joshua's Tire Centre. It felt to him as though that tire shop was an extension of Shelton Saunderson since had he not gone there to fix his flat tire that day, he would probably have given up his new job and moved back to Spruce River months ago. "Joshua is another great man," he thought. This time there were no tears. Instead, he smiled with pride that a man as great as Joshua would take the time to help him in his time of need. He was ever so proud of the friendship that had developed between the two of them.

"So now it is time for me to put all of my learning to good use," he thought to himself. "I need to start making things happen around here!"

His vision was clear in his mind and he felt that success at Shelton Saunderson was his destiny.

Chapter 15

The End

Walter immediately set about making his office everything he knew it could be. Over the next few weeks, he had many meetings with his managers in order to assure that he had the right people in management and that they understood his vision and had the ability and desire to carry it out.

Walter had to terminate one of his front line managers when during an interview, he expressed repeatedly that his direct reports were all *stupid*. Despite a series of questions intended to draw him out of his negativity, he stood his ground. He was intent that nobody in his department was capable of doing their job, and never would be. This was a fifteen person department where most of the staff were well experienced and where all of them had been with Shelton Saunderson for at least five years. Walter knew their performance levels and had confirmed with other managers that their work habits and attitudes were good. Even after a warning that his negative behavior was not appropriate, the supervisor insisted that he was right. Walter tried offering him a different position where he would have no supervisory responsibilities, but he refused. In the end, he felt it best for the firm to pay this unhappy, toxic man a fair severance and terminate him immediately. The employees in the department were thrilled with this powerful, proactive move by Walter.

Another manager, when faced with the responsibility of thinking for himself and having to provide clear expectations to his staff, voluntarily stepped down to a lesser position. He explained to Walter that he was never really comfortable in management and only had the job because at the time he was appointed, there was no one else available with the necessary qualifications. Because he was introverted and afraid of confrontation, he preferred to work in a supportive role behind the scenes while allowing someone else to manage the department. Walter made his wish come true.

Once he had the right managers in place he began teaching them the principles he had learned from Josh. He also worked with them to develop a unified vision for the company. All of them bought in completely and in no time, employees throughout the company were feeling the difference. This was a new company and everyone could see that positive change was finally happening. Walter felt good inside. Not only did he see the light at the end of the tunnel, he could feel its warmth.

The next step was to provide his managers with

financial information and encourage them to share the appropriate sections of it with their staff. He presented the most recent statements of income and expense at a special manager's meeting. He projected the statements on the boardroom screen while explaining the items line by line. The management team was impressed, both with the statistics themselves and the fact that Walter had kept his promise. They could see at a glance where the problem areas were and where improvement was needed.

Rick Rogers felt the need to speak again. This time it was all positive. "Wow, Walter! I have to say that you really came through for us. You have given us clear expectations and helped us become better managers. Now you have put the icing on the cake, by giving us the final piece of the puzzle. We have lacked this financial information for so long and it is wonderful to finally know what goes on around here. This is just great and I am officially withdrawing my challenge to you. There is no way that I want you to resign now, my friend. You may very well be the best thing that has ever happened to this company!"

With that, Rick put his hands together and began clapping slowly, then gradually accelerating the pulse. The rest of managers began clapping along with Rick and soon they all stood up, still applauding. This was the first standing ovation that any manager had ever received at Shelton Saunderson. Walter was moved to tears.

When the applause had subsided and he composed himself, Walter laughed at his show of emotion while swearing the group to secrecy. They must never let Craig Ferguson know that he had wept at a manager's meeting.

They all laughed. Walter adjourned the meeting sending them all back to work. As they walked out the door he yelled after them, "Remember folks, *If it ain't fun, it ain't worth doing!*"

All he heard in response was laughter and joyful chatter as they disappeared into their respective departments. At that moment he knew his plan was working and his vision was beginning to take shape.

The next morning when Walter approached his office door, Karla let him know that Craig Ferguson wanted to see him in his office right away. Walter immediately assumed that Craig had heard the good news about the ovation he had received at the manager's meeting and wanted to congratulate him. He strode triumphantly into Craig's office with a big grin on his face.

Craig was sitting behind his desk looking down at a memo that he was pretending to read.

"Hi Craig!" Walter said with a smile in his voice.

Without responding to Walter's greeting, Craig peered over his glasses, eyeing the younger man with the look of an angry owl. Walter immediately sensed that something was terribly wrong.

"Walter, I have a very disturbing memo on my desk," Craig said with virtually no tone in his voice. Then he raised his head and looked squarely into Walter's eyes with a pained expression on his face.

"For God's sake, Craig what is all the mystery about? What's going on?" Walter asked pleadingly. A flood of thoughts raced through Walter's mind. He wondered if maybe the financial results of the Company were not improving fast enough for the Board and maybe they were unhappy. He wondered if he had offended a staff member somehow and perhaps they had complained about him. He remembers seeing Henrietta Saunderson in the hallway a couple of days ago and even though she congratulated him on the job he was doing, she didn't seem overly friendly. "Maybe she doesn't like me," He thought. None of these thoughts were even close to the mark.

"Walter, it has come to the attention of the Board that yesterday you provided all of our managers with the year to date financial statistics of this company. I have confirmed it with Rick Rogers and some of the others so please don't try to deny it," Craig stated dryly.

"Guilty as charged, Craig. It is my opinion that our managers need that information in order to do their jobs and I intend to provide it to them every month. I gather from your tone, that you don't agree with my methodology," Walter said firmly.

"Walter, let's not play games here. You should know by now that we don't share our financials with line managers or staff, but despite that you went ahead and did it. This is not a subject for debate. I am here to tell you that this must never happen again. Furthermore, I am writing you up and a warning letter will be placed in your personnel file for future reference. Sorry my friend but this is a permanent black mark on your record with us."

Walter had not taken a seat since he entered Craig's office. As he stood in front of Craig he felt the blood drain out of his face as his body began to tremble slightly. He knew that he had to sit down. He was losing strength in his legs and he was afraid he might collapse. Once he was seated firmly on Craig's comfortable leather couch, his mind began to race again and he realized that he had a potentially life altering decision to make. In a short few seconds, he made up his mind.

Walter's voice trembled as he began speaking. "Craig, when I took this job I made a pledge to you that I would work hard and I also made a pledge to myself that I would do my best. Since then, I made an even more important pledge to the managers that if I could not fulfill my mandate of clear expectations and a transparent management environment, I would resign. I am telling you now that I fully intend to keep that promise. If you prevent me from doing what I know is right, I will have no choice but to part-company with Shelton Saunderson." Walter stopped speaking as abruptly as he began. He stared challengingly at Craig while beginning to hyperventilate.

Craig took no time in responding, "Walter, Walter, Walter, it's not the end of the world and certainly no reason to resign. Henrietta and the rest of them upstairs are just trying to make a point. They don't like sharing financial information and they want me to write you up to prove that they have sent a clear message that this bad behavior will not be tolerated. The letter is a formality. All you have to do is toe the line and, and all is forgiven. Now, why don't you just go back to work and put this behind you?"

"It's not going to happen, Craig!" Walter stated firmly and loudly. "If you won't let me do my job the way I *need* to do it, I am out of here!" Walter could barely believe that he had uttered those words. When he woke up this morning he was on top of the world. Suddenly his life was flying through space and hurtling toward the earth like a meteorite that had caught an edge on gravity. His mind was racing again as he speculated on what his next move might be. His thoughts were interrupted by Craig's voice.

"I wish you would reconsider, Walter. However, if you won't play ball with us I will have to ask you for your resignation," Craig said pleadingly.

He heard Craig's words, but he could not believe what was happening. All he had worked for. All he had accomplished. It was all gone now. None of it mattered. He knew at that moment that his career at Shelton Saunderson had come to a sudden and tragic end. Walter stood up, looked into Craig's eyes, and calmly said, "I'll clean out my desk and be gone in a few minutes." With that simple statement it was all over.

Craig shook his head as Walter walked through the doorway of his office and into the hallway. He did nothing to try to stop him and he did not call after him. He knew that like so many managers before him, even if he delayed his departure today Walter would not last in the oppressive environment that was the norm at Shelton Saunderson. "God, I can hardly wait until I can collect my pension and get out of this crazy place," Craig muttered to himself.

Chapter 16

A New Beginning

As Walter drove away from the Shelton Saunderson building, his mind went blank. He felt the tears in eyes, but he did not know why. He was neither happy nor sad; neither angry nor depressed. He felt only the same inexplicable emptiness that haunted him the day his parents took him to his grandfather's funeral. He was five years old when he had to endure that first unsettling loss. Then and now he knew that something was terribly wrong but the reality of it would not overcome his psyche until long after the event. He had suffered the loss of something very important to him but he could not fully process it at the time because his mind would not allow him to immediately accept it. In both cases, he would only understand the loss and consciously react to it weeks later. A trauma of that magnitude needs time to ferment in the soul before it can overwhelm thought and polarize emotions.

    The only thing that Walter was certain of was that he needed to work. He had a large mortgage on his new house and Lydia was not working. The monthly bills would soon become more than he could handle.

    "How will we survive?" he thought. "How will I explain this to Lydia? How will I tell my parents?" His mind was awash with negativity. He became obsessed with finding a solution to this unexpected and shocking new challenge. He thought of Joshua O'Hare fleetingly, but put the thought of visiting him out of his mind immediately. "How can I see Josh now after everything that happened today?" he thought. He felt that he had let Josh down and did not want to suffer the embarrassment of admitting his failure.

    As he pulled into the driveway of his home he was mentally rehearsing what he would say to Lydia. None of the ideas he came up with for breaking the news made the reality any less disturbing. He decided to simply say what he needed to say quickly and bluntly.

    Lydia met him in the foyer as he opened the front door. "How come you are home so early, Honey?" she asked with a smile. Walter began to tremble again, knowing that he had to tell her now. Lydia could see that something was bothering Walter, but she remained silent, waiting for his response. She was afraid of what he might say. It was only ten o'clock in the morning and Walter had never been home that early in all the years she had known him.

    "This was not a very good day, Lydia," he said calmly. "In fact, this has been the worst day of my life. I quit my job today." His voiced trailed off as he made his admission. His top lip was quivering as he looked into Lydia's eyes. Instinctively he stepped toward his wife and embraced her. He could feel her body immediately curve into him in a gesture of support. They held each other for a few seconds that seemed like an eternity without speaking. Finally Lydia broke the silence.

"Do you want to talk about it, Walter?" Lydia asked softly. He did not reply.

She took him by the hand and led him into their comfortable living room. When he was settled into his favorite chair, she went to the kitchen and poured two cups of coffee. When she brought the hot, steaming cups into the living room, he began telling his story. He told her everything that had happened that day and filled her in on some of the events that had occurred over the past few months that brought him to this end. He talked for over an hour as she listened intently. She did not speak, only nodding and offering inaudible approval from time to time. Lydia had always been a great listener.

When he was done speaking, Walter looked into Lydia's eyes for approval. "So did I do the right thing?" he asked.

"Absolutely!" She yelled. "I am so proud of you right now that I feel like running down the street hollering, **Walter Kennedy is the greatest man in the world!**"

That brought a smile to Walter's face. Smiling felt good to him after the day he had. "So really Honey, what should I do now?" he asked sincerely.

"You really need to take some time to think, Walter. Don't do anything rash or impetuous just because you have lost your job. We will be fine for a while and I am sure that you will land on your feet. I think you ought to go see your friend, Josh down at the tire shop. He hasn't steered you too far wrong yet. He might have some good ideas and anyway, it can't hurt." Lydia said confidently.

Lydia knew that Walter admired Joshua O'Hare and that he could offer the kind of comfort and affirmation that she could not. She understood that business relationships and marriage relationships are equally important but very different. She knew instinctively that even though Walter was happy in the knowledge that she was fully supportive of his decision, he needed to hear it from someone else.

Walter looked at his watch. Seeing that it was eleven thirty, he knew he could make it to Joshua's Tire Center just in time to catch Josh before lunch. Josh usually ate at his desk, so Walter was confident that he would be there. As he backed out of his driveway and headed toward the tire shop, he wondered how Josh would take the news.

As he entered *"Joshua's Tires,"* Karen sensed that there was something different about Walter that day. "Hi, Mr. Kennedy…Are you okay? Can I get you anything?" she asked genuinely.

"No thanks, Karen. Can I go in the back and see Josh?" he asked politely.

"Sure, go ahead. I think he is doing the books back there today and he would probably like a break," she said with a wink.

When Josh saw him drawing near his office door he also sensed the change in Walter and it made him nervous. He knew that Walter had been pushing his new business model very hard at Shelton Saunderson and he hoped it hadn't caused him any undue distress. His worst fears were soon realized.

After exchanging greetings and embracing briefly, Walter unloaded on Josh. "Craig Ferguson gave me the option of toeing the company line or resigning today, and I chose the latter," he said. Walter could see the sudden look of dismay and concern on Josh's face, so he quickly added, "I think it's for the best, Josh. They really didn't like my ideas anyway."

Josh had to sit back in chair for a moment and absorb what he had just heard. He felt almost completely responsible for Walter having lost his job, but in a way he was glad that it had happened. He knew that Shelton Saunderson needed a good shake up and he knew that Walter might just be the one to do it. He now hoped that Walter's resignation might send a message to Craig and the Board that it was time for a change. He also knew that this was his opportunity to get Walter on board at "Joshua's Tire Centers".

"My God Walter, tell me what happened. I hope it wasn't one of my ideas that caused it," Josh said in a very serious tone.

Still standing, Walter said, "No Josh. It wasn't your advice that caused it at all. In fact, it was something that I went ahead and did even though you warned me not to do it. I gave the managers the financial information that Shelton Saunderson had always withheld, and the Board absolutely *lost it*. They insisted that I never do it again and I told Craig that I would not toe that line. It was a very short meeting really. It was almost like everything else I did there never happened at all. I walked out of his office without even saying goodbye to anyone…and I never looked back."

Hearing no response from Josh, Walter asked weakly, "So what do you think of me now?"

Feeling Walter's pain, Josh leaped from his chair and embraced the younger man. That brought a wave of emotion to Walter that he could no longer control. He broke down in tears saying, "I'm so sorry, Josh. I know I let you down."

When the two men broke their embrace, Josh said sympathetically, "Walter my dear friend, you have never let me down. You have one of the greatest business minds I have ever come across and I only wish I were lucky enough to have a bright young guy like you running my company. Those Shelton Saunderson characters will soon learn what they have lost in you."

Suddenly Walter's mind focussed on Josh's comment. "Is he asking me to run *Joshua's Tire Centers*?" he wondered. At that moment, the other times when Josh seemed to be suggesting that he should come to work at the tire shop came flooding into his mind. Now it all made sense. This was his future and this was where he must stay. He quickly put Shelton Saunderson out of his mind as thoughts of the tire business danced across his consciousness.

"Josh to you mean it? Do you really want me to run your company?" Walter asked.

"You bet, son. I want to start taking some time off and I need a good Chief Operations Officer. I am thinking that I could stay on as the CEO until you get the hang of things but you would be the President of the company and you would be responsible for virtually everything that goes on around here. We can hammer out a compensation package that will make certain that You, Lydia and the kids are well taken care of. Darn it, Walter, I just think this could be a Heck of a lot of fun for both of us." Josh had a big smile on his face and his head was cocked to the side in an inquisitive stance.

Walter felt a certain calmness now that he had not felt since he left Spruce River. He knew that this would be his destiny and his legacy. He wasted no time in accepting Josh's offer.

"Well, Josh if you think you can make a COO out of failed insurance manager like me, then who am I to say no?" Walter asked playfully. He was so happy that he could hardly contain himself "When do I start?" he asked before throwing his arms around Josh again in a joyful embrace.

"Well, Walt. How about we go down to Kiroshi's place for lunch and talk about it?" Josh asked.

"Sounds good to me, Josh," Walter responded with a laugh. He realized then that he couldn't stop smiling and laughing. He had finally reached his goal. He had finally found the right job for him and he was about to have more fun than he had ever had in his life.

As the two men walked out into the parking lot at *Joshua's Tire Center*, Josh directed Walter to the red, 1963 split window Corvette that he admired so much. As they approached the car, Josh reached into his pocket, pulled out the keys and handed them to Walter. Unsure of what to do, Walter looked at Josh for a moment and then asked, "What's up, Josh?"

"Well, Walter. I have a few other cars and I know how much you like this one, so let's just call this your signing bonus. This is your car now. If you treat her well, she should give you many years of driving pleasure." Josh said with a smile.

"Jeez, Josh. I can't take your car," Walter said emphatically. "I know how much work you put into it."

"You are going to do a lot more work for me over the next few years than I put into that car, so take the keys and let's go for lunch. And, by the way Walter, don't argue with the boss. You know the trouble that can get you into!" Josh said with a laugh.

As he slid into the driver's seat and started the engine, Walter said, "Okay, Josh I am not going to argue anymore. This started out to be the worst day of my life and it has turned into the best day of my life. I am really having fun now." He suddenly giggled and with a twinkle in his eye he asked," Hey, Josh. do you remember what my Dad used to say?"

"You bet young fella...Let's say it together like we mean it!" Josh yelled as the big V8 engine roared.

As the Corvette sped out of the parking lot the two men could be heard shouting in unison, *"If it ain't fun, it ain't worth doing!"*

Karen and the other staff in the shop all laughed to hear the two of them. No one could remember ever seeing Josh quite so happy.

Walter spent the rest of his working life as COO and eventually CEO of Joshua's Tire Centers. Under this leadership the firm grew into the largest tire retailer in the Nation. Even though he wasn't initially keen on the idea, Walter also expanded the firm into Europe, as Joshua had always wanted. Despite his concerns it became one of their largest and most profitable divisions.

Joshua stayed on for three years after Walter took over as President. He was pleased with how quickly Walter learned the business and he soon learned that his leadership abilities were even better than he had hoped.

Knowing that his company was safe, Josh purchased a house near the ocean and retired there with his wife of 35 years. The day after his retirement party, Josh sat alone on the porch of his beachside home, while the sights and sounds of the ocean mesmerized him. As he was slowly lulled to sleep by the crashing waves and the serenity of his surroundings, he thought to himself, "It is so true…*If it ain't fun, it ain't worth doing!*"

The End for me…
A New Beginning for you.
Wayne Kehl

For more information about Wayne Kehl,
his services, or where to order more books, visit:
www.waynekehl.com